OLD MOORE'S

HOROSCOPE AND ASTRAL DIARY

CANCER

OLD MOORE'S

HOROSCOPE AND ASTRAL DIARY

CANCER

foulsham
LONDON · NEW YORK · TORONTO · SYDNEY

foulsham

Capital Point, 33 Bath Road, Slough, Berkshire, SL1 3UF, England

Foulsham books can be found in all good bookshops and direct from
www.foulsham.com

ISBN: 978-0-572-03655-3

A CIP record for this book is available from the British Library

Printed in Great Britain by Cox & Wyman Ltd, Reading, Berkshire.

CONTENTS

INTRODUCTION

Astrology has been with us for a very long time and our fascination for the starry heavens seems to go back many thousands of years. Incised bones carrying lunar calendars have been found that are tens of thousands of years old, and our belief that the stars and planets have a bearing on our daily lives could easily be almost as ancient. Astrology was studied in all the major civilisations, and shows no signs of diminishing in popularity in the 21st century. Old Moore, a time-served veteran in astrological research, continues to monitor the zodiac and has produced the Astral Diary for 2012, tailor-made to your own astrological make-up.

Old Moore's Astral Diary is unique in its ability to get the heart of your nature and to offer you the sort of advice that might come from a trusted friend. The Diaries are structured in such a way that you can see in a day-by-day sense exactly how the planets are working for you. The diary section advises how you can get the best from upcoming situations and allows you to plan ahead successfully. There is room in the daily sections to put your own observations or even appointments, and the book is conveniently structured to stay with you throughout the year.

Whilst other popular astrology books merely deal with your astrological Sun sign, the Astral Diaries go much further. Every person on the planet is unique, and Old Moore allows you to access your individuality in a number of ways. The front section gives you the chance to work out the placement of the Moon at the time of your birth and to see how its position has set an important seal on your overall nature. Perhaps most important of all, you can use the Astral Diary to discover your Rising sign. This is the zodiac sign that was appearing over the Eastern horizon at the time of your birth, and is just as important to you as an individual as is your Sun sign.

It is the synthesis of many different astrological possibilities that makes you what you are, and with the Astral Diaries you can learn so much. How do you react to love and romance? Through the unique Venus tables and the readings that follow them, you can learn where the planet Venus was at the time of your birth. It is even possible to register when little Mercury is 'retrograde', which means that it appears to be moving backwards in space when viewed from the Earth. Mercury rules communication, so be prepared to deal with a few setbacks in this area when you see the sign ☿. The Astral Diary will be an interest and a support throughout the whole year ahead.

Old Moore extends his customary greeting to all people of the Earth and offers his age-old wishes for a happy and prosperous period ahead.

THE ESSENCE
OF CANCER

Exploring the Personality of
Cancer the Crab

(22nd JUNE – 22nd JULY)

What's in a sign?

The most obvious fact about you, particularly when viewed by others, is that you are trustworthy. Sometimes this fact gets on your nerves. Many Cancerians long to be bigger, bolder and more ruthless, but it simply isn't the way you were made. You are basically ruled by your emotions and there is very little you can do to get away from the fact. Once you realise this you could be in for a happy life but there are bound to be some frustrations on the way.

Your ruling planet is the Moon, which changes its position in astrological terms far more quickly than any other heavenly body. That's why you can sometimes feel that you have experienced a whole year's emotions in only a month. However the saving grace of this fact is that unlike the other Water signs of Scorpio and Pisces, you are rarely bogged down by emotional restraints for more than a day or two at a time. This gives you a more optimistic attitude and a determination to use your natural talents to the full, even in the face of some adversity. Caring for others is second nature to you and forms a very large part of your life and character.

Your attitude towards romance fluctuates but is generally of the 'story book' sort. Once you commit yourself to another person, either romantically or practically, you are not likely to change your mind very easily. Loyalty is part of what you are about and doesn't change just because things sometimes get a little complicated. Even when you don't really know where you are going, you are inclined to pull those you love along the path with you, and you can usually rely on their assistance. Basically you are very easy to love and there can't be anything much wrong with that fact. At the same time you can be very practical, don't mind doing some of the dirty work and are in your element when those around you are floundering.

The creative potential within your nature is strong. You are a natural homemaker and tend to get a great deal from simply watching others succeed. All the same this isn't the whole story because you are complex and inclined to be too worrisome.

Cancer resources

Your ruling planet is the Moon, Earth's closest neighbour in space. This means that you are as subject to its tides and fluctuations as is our planet. Of course this is a double-edged sword because you can sometimes be an emotional maelstrom inside. To compensate for this fact you have a level of personal sensitivity that would be admired by many. At the same time you have a deep intuition and can usually be relied upon to see through the mist of everyday life and to work out how situations are likely to mature. This is especially true when it comes to assessing those around you.

As a homemaker you are second to none. You can make a few pounds go a very long way and can cope well in circumstances that would greatly trouble those around you. Adversity is not something that bothers you too much at all and it is clear that you can even revel in difficulty. Nothing is too much trouble when you are dealing with people you really love – which includes friends as well as family members.

One of the greatest Cancerian resources is the ability to bring a practical face to even difficult circumstances. Physically speaking you are very resilient, even if you don't always seem to be the strongest person around in an emotional sense. You are given to showing extreme kindness, sometimes even in the face of cruelty from others, though if you are genuinely provoked you can show an anger that would shock most people, even those who think they know you very well indeed.

What really counts the most is your ability to bring others round to your point of view and to get them to do what you think is best. Working from example you won't generally expect others to do anything you are not prepared to try yourself, and your attitude can be an inspiration to others. Through hard work and perseverance you can build a good life for yourself, though your consideration for those around you never diminishes and so even a fortune gained would generally be used on behalf of the world around you. The greatest resource that you possess is your capacity to love and to nurture. This makes you successful and well loved by others.

Beneath the surface

The most difficult aspect of those born under the sign of Cancer the Crab is trying to work out the psychological motivations of this apparently simple but actually deeply complex zodiac position. 'Emotion' is clearly the keyword and is the fountain from which everything, good and bad alike, flows. Whilst some zodiac sign types are inclined to act and then consider the consequences, the Crab is a different beast altogether. The main quality of Cancer is caring. This applies as much to the world at large as it does in consideration of family, though to the Crab it's clear that under almost all circumstances family comes first.

You are a deep thinker and don't always find it easy to explain the way your mind is working. The reason for this is not so difficult to understand. Feelings are not the same as thoughts and it is sometimes quite difficult to express the qualities that rule you internally. What you seem to prefer to do is to put a caring arm around the world and express your inner compassion in this manner. You might also sometimes be a little anxious that if others knew how your innermost mind worked you would become more vulnerable than you already are – which is why the Crab wears a shell in the first place.

At the first sign of emotional pressure from outside you are inclined to retreat into yourself. As a result you don't always confront issues that would be best dealt with immediately. This proclivity runs deep and strong in your nature and can sometimes cause you much more trouble than would be the case if you just made the right statements and asked the correct questions. Physically and mentally you are not inclined to withdraw because you are very much stronger than the world would give you credit for.

Cancerians have a tremendous capacity to love, allied to a potential for positive action when the lives or well-being of others is threatened. In some ways you are the bravest zodiac sign of all because you will march forward into the very gates of hell if you know that you can be of service to those around you. From family to village or town, from town to nation and from nation to a global awareness, yours is the zodiac sign that best epitomises humanity's struggle for a universal understanding.

Making the best of yourself

If you start out from the premise that you are well liked by most people then you are halfway towards any intended destination. Of course you don't always register your popularity and are given to worrying about the impression you give. The picture you paint of yourself is usually very different from the one the world at large sees. If you doubt this, ask some of your best friends to describe your nature and you will be quite surprised. You need to be as open as possible to avoid internalising matters that would be best brought into a more public arena. Your natural tendency to look after everyone else masks a desire to get on in life personally, and the Cancerians who succeed the best are the ones who have somehow managed to bring a sense of balance to their giving and taking.

Try to avoid being too quiet. In social situations you have much to offer, though would rarely do so in a particularly gregarious manner. Nevertheless, and partly because you don't shoot your mouth off all the time, people are willing to listen to what you have to say. Once you realise how strong your influence can be you are already on the road to riches – financial and personal.

Use your imagination to the full because it is one of the most potent weapons in your personal armoury. People won't underestimate you when they know how strong you really are and that means that life can sometimes be less of a struggle. But under most circumstances be your usual warm self, and the love you desire will come your way.

The very practical issues of life are easy for you to deal with, which is why your material success is generally assured. All that is needed to make the picture complete is more confidence in your ability to lead and less inclination to follow.

The impressions you give

There is no doubt at all that you are one of the most loved and the most admired people around. It isn't hard to see why. Your relatives and friends alike feel very protected and loved, which has got to be a good start when it comes to your contacts with the world at large.

The most intriguing thing about being a Cancerian subject is how different you appear to be when viewed by others as against the way you judge your own personality. This is down to external appearances as much as anything. For starters you usually wear a cheery smile, even on those occasions when it is clear you are not smiling inside. You give yourself fully to the needs and wants of those around you and are very sympathetic, even towards strangers. It's true that you may not fully exploit the implications of your pleasant nature – but that's only another typical part of your character.

Those people who know you the best are aware that you have a great capacity to worry about things, and they may also understand that you are rarely as confident as you give the external impression of being. They sense the deeply emotional quality of your nature and can observe the long periods of deep thought. When it comes to the practicalities of life, however, you perhaps should not be surprised that you are sometimes put on rather too much. Even this is understandable because you rarely say no and will usually make yourself available when there is work to be done.

True success for the Cancer subject lies in recognising your strong points and in being willing to gain from them in a personal sense from time to time. You also need to realise that, to others, the impression you give is what you really are. Bridging the gap between outward calm and inner confusion might be the most important lesson.

The way forward

Although you don't always feel quite as sure of yourself as you give the impression of being, you can still exploit your external appearance to your own and other people's advantage. Your strong sense of commitment to family and your ability to get on well in personal relationships are both factors that improve your ability to progress in life.

Achieving a sense of balance is important. For example you can spend long hours locked into your own thoughts, but this isn't good for you in an exclusive sense. Playing out some of your fantasies in the real world can do you good, even though you are aware that this involves taking chances, something you don't always care to do. At the same time you should not be afraid to make gains as a result of the way you are loved by others. This doesn't come for free and you work long and hard to establish the affection that comes your way.

In practical matters you are capable and well able to get on in life. Money comes your way, not usually as a result of particularly good luck, but because you are a tireless and steady worker. You can accept responsibility, even though the implied management side of things worries you somewhat. To have a career is important because it broadens your outlook and keeps you functioning in the wider world, which is where your personal successes take place. The more you achieve, the greater is the level of confidence that you feel – which in turn leads to even greater progress.

Cancerians should never cut themselves off from the mainstream of life. It's true you have many acquaintances but very few really close friends, but that doesn't matter. Practically everyone you know is pleased to name you as a trusted ally, which has to be the best compliment of all to your apparently serene and settled nature.

In love you are ardent and sincere. It may take you a while to get round to expressing the way you feel, partly because you are a little afraid of failure in this most important area of your life. All the same you love with a passion and are supportive to your partner. Family will always be the most important sphere of life because your zodiac sign rules the astrological fourth house, which is essentially dedicated to home and family matters. If you are contented in this arena it tends to show in other areas of your life too. Your affable nature is your best friend and only tends to disappear if you allow yourself to become too stressed.

CANCER ON THE CUSP

Old Moore is often asked how astrological profiles are altered for those people born at either the beginning or the end of a zodiac sign, or, more properly, on the cusps of a sign. In the case of Cancer this would be on the 22nd of June and for two or three days after, and similarly at the end of the sign, probably from the 20th to the 22nd of July. In this year's Astral Diaries, once again, Old Moore sets out to explain the differences regarding cuspid signs.

The Gemini Cusp – June 22nd to June 24th

You are certainly fun to be around and the sign of Gemini has a great deal to do with your basic motivations. As a result, you tend to be slightly more chatty than the average Cancerian and usually prove to be the life and soul of any party that is going on in your vicinity. Not everyone understands the basic sensitivity that lies below the surface of this rather brash exterior, however, and you can sometimes be a little hurt if people take you absolutely at face value.

There probably isn't the total consistency of emotional responses that one generally expects to find in the Crab when taken alone, and there are times when you might be accused of being rather fickle. All the same, you have a big heart and show genuine concern for anyone in trouble, especially the underdog. Your Gemini attributes give you the opportunity to speak your mind, so when it comes to aiding the world you can be a tireless reformer and show a great ability to think before you speak, which is not typical of Gemini on its own, although there are occasions when the two sides of your nature tend to be at odds with each other.

At work you are very capable and can be relied upon to make instant decisions whenever necessary. Your executive capabilities are pronounced and you are more than capable of thinking on your feet, even if you prefer to mull things over if possible. You are the sort of person that others tend to rely on for advice and will not usually let your colleagues or friends down.

In matters of love, you are less steadfast and loyal than the Crab, yet you care very deeply for your loved ones. People like to have you around and actively seek your advice which, in the main, is considered and sound, though always delivered with humour. You love to travel and would never wish to be limited in either your horizons or your lifestyle. All in all, you are a fun person, good to know, and basically sensible.

The Leo Cusp – July 20th to July 22nd

Here we find a Cancerian who tends to know what he or she wants from life. Part of the natural tendency of the Crab is to be fairly shy and retiring, though progressively less so as the Sun moves on towards the sign of Leo. You are probably aware that you don't exactly match the Cancer stereotype and are likely to be more outspoken, determined and even argumentative at times. You have lofty ideals, which find a ready home for the sensitive qualities that you draw from Cancer. Many social reformers tend to have their Suns very close to the Leo cusp of Cancer and people born on this cusp like to work hard for the world, especially for the less well-off members of society.

In matters of love, you are deep, but ardent and sincere, finding better ways of expressing your emotions verbally than those generally associated with the Crab. You are capable at work, easily able to take on responsibilities that involve controlling other people, and you are outwardly braver than often seems to be the case with Cancer alone. Not everyone finds you particularly easy to understand, probably because there are some definite paradoxes about your nature.

A few problems come along in the area of ideals, which are more important to you than they would be to some of the people with whom you associate. You need to be sure of yourself, a fact that leads to fairly long thinking periods, but once you have formed a particular belief you will move heaven and earth to demonstrate how sensible it is. Don't be too alarmed if not everyone agrees with you.

You are not the typical conformist that might more usually be the case with Cancerians, and feel the need to exercise your civic rights to the full. Tireless when dealing with something you think is especially important, you are a good and loyal friend, a staunch and steadfast lover and you care deeply about your family. However, you are not as confrontational as a person born completely under Leo, and therefore can usually be relied upon to seek a compromise.

CANCER AND ITS ASCENDANTS

The nature of every individual on the planet is composed of the rich variety of zodiac signs and planetary positions that were present at the time of their birth. Your Sun sign, which in your case is Cancer, is one of the many factors when it comes to assessing the unique person you are. Probably the most important consideration, other than your Sun sign, is to establish the zodiac sign that was rising over the eastern horizon at the time that you were born. This is your Ascending or Rising sign. Most popular astrology fails to take account of the Ascendant, and yet its importance remains with you from the very moment of your birth, through every day of your life. The Ascendant is evident in the way you approach the world, and so, when meeting a person for the first time, it is this astrological influence that you are most likely to notice first. Our Ascending sign essentially represents what we appear to be, while the Sun sign is what we feel inside ourselves.

The Ascendant also has the potential for modifying our overall nature. For example, if you were born at a time of day when Cancer was passing over the eastern horizon (this would be around the time of dawn) then you would be classed as a double Cancerian. As such, you would typify this zodiac sign, both internally and in your dealings with others. However, if your Ascendant sign turned out to be a Fire sign, such as Aries, there would be a profound alteration of nature, away from the expected qualities of Cancer.

One of the reasons why popular astrology often ignores the Ascendant is that it has always been rather difficult to establish. Old Moore has found a way to make this possible by devising an easy-to-use table, which you will find on page 159 of this book. Using this, you can establish your Ascendant sign at a glance. You will need to know your rough time of birth, then it is simply a case of following the instructions.

For those readers who have no idea of their time of birth it might be worth allowing a good friend, or perhaps your partner, to read through the section that follows this introduction. Someone who deals with you on a regular basis may easily discover your Ascending sign, even though you could have some difficulty establishing it for yourself. A good understanding of this component of your nature is essential if you want to be aware of that 'other person' who is responsible for the way you make contact with the world at large. Your Sun sign, Ascendant sign, and the other pointers in this book will, together, allow you a far better understanding of what makes you tick as an individual. Peeling back the different layers of your astrological make-up can be an enlightening experience, and the Ascendant may represent one of the most important layers of all.

Cancer with Cancer Ascendant

You are one of the most warm and loving individuals that it is possible to know, and you carry a quiet dignity that few would fail to recognise. Getting on with things in your own steady way, you are, nevertheless, capable of great things, simply because you keep going. Even in the face of adversity your steady but relentless pace can be observed, and much of what you do is undertaken on behalf of those you love the most. On the other side of the coin you represent something of a mystery and it is also true that emotionally speaking you tend to be very highly charged. It doesn't take much to bring you to tears and you are inclined to have a special affection for the underdog, which on occasions can get you into a little trouble. Although it is your natural way to keep a low profile, you will speak out loudly if you think that anyone you care for is under attack, and yet you don't show the same tendency on your own behalf.

Rarely if ever out of control, you are the levelling influence everyone feels they need in their life, which is one of the reasons why you are so loved. Your quiet ways are accepted by the world, which is why some people will be astonished when you suddenly announce that you are about to travel overland to Asia. What a great puzzle you can be, but that is half the attraction.

Cancer with Leo Ascendant

This can be a very fortunate combination, for when seen at its best it brings all the concern and the natural caring qualities of Cancer, allied to the more dynamic and very brave face of Leo. Somehow there is a great deal of visible energy here, but it manifests itself in a way that always shows a concern for the world at large. No matter what charitable works are going on in your district it is likely that you will be involved in one way or another, and you relish the cut and thrust of life much more than the the retiring side of Cancer would seem to do. You are quite capable of walking alone and don't really need the company of others for large chunks of the average day. However, when you are in social situations you fare very well and can usually be observed with a smile on your face.

Conversationally speaking you have sound, considered opinions and often represent the voice of steady wisdom when faced with a situation that means arbitration. In fact you will often be put in this situation, and there is more than one politician and union representative who shares this undeniably powerful zodiac combination. Like all those associated with the sign of Cancer you love to travel and can make a meal out of your journeys with brave, intrepid Leo lending a hand in both the planning and the doing.

Cancer with Virgo Ascendant

What can this union of zodiac signs bring to the party that isn't there in either Cancer or Virgo alone? Well, quite a bit actually. Virgo can be very fussy on occasions and too careful for its own good. The presence of steady, serene Cancer alters the perspectives and allows a smoother, more flowing individual to greet the world. You are chatty and easy to know, and exhibit a combination of the practical skills of Virgo, together with the deep and penetrating insights that are typical of Cancer. This can make you appear to be very powerful and your insights are second to none. You are a born organiser and love to be where things are happening, even if you are only there to help make the sandwiches or to pour the tea. Invariably your role will be much greater but you don't seek personal acclaim and are a good team player on most occasions.

There is a quiet side to your nature and those who live with you will eventually get used to your need for solitude. This seems strange because Virgo is generally such a chatterbox and, taken on its own, is rarely quiet for long. In matters of love you show great affection and a sense of responsibility that makes you an ideal parent. It is sometimes the case, however, that you care rather more than you should be willing to show.

Cancer with Libra Ascendant

What an absolutely pleasant and approachable sort of person you are, and how much you have to offer. Like most people associated with the sign of Cancer, you give yourself freely to the world and will always be on hand if anyone is in trouble or needs the special touch you can bring to almost any problem. Behaving in this way is the biggest part of what you are and so people come to rely on you very heavily. Like Libra you can see both sides of any coin and you exhibit the Libran tendency to jump about from one foot to the other when it is necessary to make decisions relating to your own life. This is not usually the case when you are dealing with others, however, because the cooler and more detached qualities of Cancer will show through in these circumstances.

It would be fair to say that you do not deal with routines as well as Cancer alone might do and you need a degree of variety in your life. In your case this possibly comes in the form of travel, which can be distant and of long duration. It isn't unusual for people who have this zodiac combination to end up living abroad, though even this does little to prevent you from getting itchy feet from time to time. In relationships you show an original quality that keeps the relationship young, fresh and working well.

Cancer with Scorpio Ascendant

There are few more endearing zodiac combinations than this. Both signs are Watery in nature and show a desire to work on behalf of humanity as a whole. The world sees you as being genuinely caring, full of sympathy for anyone in trouble and always ready to lend a hand when it is needed. You are a loyal friend, a great supporter of the oppressed and a lover of home and family. In a work sense you are capable and command respect from your colleagues, even though this comes about courtesy of your quiet competence, and not as a result of anything that you might happen to say or do.

But we should not get too carried away with external factors, or the way that others see you. Inside you are a boiling pool of emotion. You feel more strongly, love more deeply and hurt more fully than any other combination of the Water signs. Even those who think that they know you really well would get a shock if they could take a stroll around the deeper recesses of your mind. Although these facts are true, they may be rather beside the point because the truth of your passion, commitment and deep convictions may only surface fully half a dozen times in your life. The fact is that you are a very private person at heart and you don't know how to be any other way.

Cancer with Sagittarius Ascendant

You have far more drive, enthusiasm and get-up-and-go than would seem to be the case for Cancer when taken alone, but all of this is tempered with a certain quiet compassion that probably makes you the best sort of Sagittarian too. It's true that you don't like to be on your own or to retire into your shell quite as much as the Crab usually does, though there are, even in your case, occasions when this is going to be necessary. Absolute concentration can sometimes be a problem to you, though this is hardly likely to be the case when you are dealing with matters relating to your home or family, both of which reign supreme in your thinking. Always loving and kind, you are a social animal and enjoy being out there in the real world, expressing the deeper opinions of Cancer much more readily than would often be the case with other combinations relating to the sign of the Crab.

Personality is not lacking, and you tend to be very popular, not least because you are the fountain of good and practical advice. You want to get things done, and retain a practical approach to most situations which is the envy of many of the people you meet. As a parent you are second to none, combining common sense, dignity and a sensible approach. To balance this you stay young enough to understand children.

Cancer with Capricorn Ascendant

The single most important factor here is the practical ability to get things done and to see any task, professional or personal, through to the end. Since half this combination is Cancer, that also means expounding much of your energy on behalf of others. There isn't a charity in the world that would fail to recognise what a potent combination this is when it comes to the very concrete side of offering help and assistance. Many of your ideas hold water and you don't set off on abortive journeys of any kind, simply because you tend to get the ground rules fixed in your mind first.

On a more personal level you can be rather hard to get to know, because both these signs have a deep quality and a tendency to keep things in the dark. The mystery may only serve to encourage people to try and get to know you better. As a result you could attract a host of admirers, many of whom would wish to form romantic attachments. This may prove to be irrelevant, however, because once you give your heart, you tend to be loyal and would only change your mind if you were pushed into doing so. Prolonged periods of inactivity don't do you any good and it is sensible for you to keep on the move, even though your progress in life is measured and very steady.

Cancer with Aquarius Ascendant

The truly original spark, for which the sign of Aquarius is famed, can only enhance the caring qualities of Cancer, and is also inclined to bring the Crab out of its shell to a much greater extent than would be the case with certain other zodiac combinations. Aquarius is a party animal and never arrives without something interesting to say, which is doubly so when the reservoir of emotion and consideration that is Cancer is feeding the tap. Your nature can be rather confusing, even for you to deal with, but you are inspirational, bright, charming and definitely fun to be around.

The Cancer element in your nature means that you care about your home and the people to whom you are related. You are also a good and loyal friend, who would keep attachments for much longer than could be expected for Aquarius alone. You love to travel and can be expected to make many journeys to far-off places during your life. Some attention will have to be paid to your health because you are capable of burning up masses of nervous energy, often without getting the periods of rest and contemplation that are essential to the deeper qualities of the sign of Cancer. Nevertheless you have determination, resilience and a refreshing attitude that lifts the spirits of the people in your vicinity.

Cancer with Pisces Ascendant

A deep, double Water-sign combination, this one, and it might serve to make you a very misunderstood, though undoubtedly popular, individual. You are keen to make a good impression, probably too keen under certain circumstances, and you do everything you can to help others, even if you don't know them very well. It's true that you are deeply sensitive and quite easily brought to tears by the suffering of this most imperfect world that we inhabit. Fatigue can be a problem, though this is nullified to some extent by the fact that you can withdraw completely into the deep recesses of your own mind when it becomes necessary to do so.

You may not be the most gregarious person in the world, simply because it isn't easy for you to put your most important considerations into words. This is easier when you are in the company of people you know and trust, though even trust is a commodity that is difficult for you to find, particularly since you may have been hurt by being too willing to share your thoughts early in life. With age comes wisdom and maturity and the older you are, the better you will learn to handle this potent and demanding combination. You will never go short of either friends or would-be lovers, and may be one of the most magnetic types of both Cancer and Pisces.

Cancer with Aries Ascendant

The main problem that you experience in life shows itself as a direct result of the meshing of these two very different zodiac signs. At heart Aries needs to dominate, whereas Cancer shows a desire to nurture. All too often the result can be a protective arm that is so strong that nobody could possibly get out from under it. Lighten your own load, and that of those you care for, by being willing to sit back and watch others please themselves a little. You might think that you know best, and your heart is clearly in the right place, but try and realise what life can be like when someone is always on hand to tell you that they know better than you do.

But in a way this is a little severe, because you are fairly intuitive and your instincts will rarely lead you astray. Nobody could ask for a better partner or parent than you would be, though they might request a slightly less attentive one. In matters of work you are conscientious, and are probably best suited to a job that means sorting out the kind of mess that humanity is so good at creating. You probably spend your spare time untangling balls of wool, though you are quite sporting too and could even make the Olympics. Once there you would not win however, because you would be too concerned about all the other competitors!

Cancer with Taurus Ascendant

Your main aim in life seems to be to look after everyone and everything that you come across. From your deepest and most enduring human love, right down to the birds in the park, you really do care and you show that natural affection in many different ways. Your nature is sensitive and you are easily moved to tears, though this does not prevent you from pitching in and doing practical things to assist at just about any level. There is a danger that you could stifle those same people whom you set out to assist, and people with this zodiac combination are often unwilling, or unable, to allow their children to grow and leave the nest. More time spent considering what suits you would be no bad thing, but the problem is that you find it almost impossible to imagine any situation that doesn't involve your most basic need, which is to nurture.

You appear not to possess a selfish streak, though it sometimes turns out that in being certain that you understand the needs of the world, you are nevertheless treading on their toes. This eventual realisation can be very painful, but it isn't a stick with which you should beat yourself because at heart you are one of the kindest people imaginable. Your sense of fair play means that you are a quiet social reformer at heart.

Cancer with Gemini Ascendant

Many astrologers would say that this is a happy combination because some of the more flighty qualities of Gemini are somewhat modified by the steady influence of Cancer the Crab. To all intents and purposes you show the friendly and gregarious qualities of Gemini, but there is a thoughtful and even sometimes a serious quality that would not be present in Gemini when taken alone. Looking after people is high on your list of priorities and you do this most of the time. This is made possible because you have greater staying power than Gemini is usually said to possess and you can easily see fairly complicated situations through to their conclusion without becoming bored on the way.

The chances are that you will have many friends and that these people show great concern for your well-being, because you choose them carefully and show them a great deal of consideration. However, you will still be on the receiving end of gossip on occasions, and need to treat such situations with a healthy pinch of salt. Like all part-Geminis your nervous system is not as strong as you would wish to believe and family pressures in particular can put great strain on you. Activities of all kinds take your fancy and many people with this combination are attracted to sailing or wind surfing.

THE MOON AND THE PART IT PLAYS IN YOUR LIFE

In astrology the Moon is probably the single most important heavenly body after the Sun. Its unique position, as partner to the Earth on its journey around the solar system, means that the Moon appears to pass through the signs of the zodiac extremely quickly. The zodiac position of the Moon at the time of your birth plays a great part in personal character and is especially significant in the build-up of your emotional nature.

Sun Moon Cycles

The first lunar cycle deals with the part the position of the Moon plays relative to your Sun sign. I have made the fluctuations of this pattern easy for you to understand by means of a simple cyclic graph. It appears on the first page of each 'Your Month At A Glance', under the title 'Highs and Lows'. The graph displays the lunar cycle and you will soon learn to understand how its movements have a bearing on your level of energy and your abilities.

Your Own Moon Sign

Discovering the position of the Moon at the time of your birth has always been notoriously difficult because tracking the complex zodiac positions of the Moon is not easy. This process has been reduced to three simple stages with Old Moore's unique Lunar Tables. A breakdown of the Moon's zodiac positions can be found from page 25 onwards, so that once you know what your Moon Sign is, you can see what part this plays in the overall build-up of your personal character.

If you follow the instructions on the next page you will soon be able to work out exactly what zodiac sign the Moon occupied on the day that you were born and you can then go on to compare the reading for this position with those of your Sun sign and your Ascendant. It is partly the comparison between these three important positions that goes towards making you the unique individual you are.

HOW TO DISCOVER YOUR MOON SIGN

This is a three-stage process. You may need a pen and a piece of paper but if you follow the instructions below the process should only take a minute or so.

STAGE 1 First of all you need to know the Moon Age at the time of your birth. If you look at Moon Table 1, on page 23, you will find all the years between 1914 and 2012 down the left side. Find the year of your birth and then trace across to the right to the month of your birth. Where the two intersect you will find a number. This is the date of the New Moon in the month that you were born. You now need to count forward the number of days between the New Moon and your own birthday. For example, if the New Moon in the month of your birth was shown as being the 6th and you were born on the 20th, your Moon Age Day would be 14. If the New Moon in the month of your birth came after your birthday, you need to count forward from the New Moon in the previous month. Whatever the result, jot this number down so that you do not forget it.

STAGE 2 Take a look at Moon Table 2 on page 24. Down the left hand column look for the date of your birth. Now trace across to the month of your birth. Where the two meet you will find a letter. Copy this letter down alongside your Moon Age Day.

STAGE 3 Moon Table 3 on page 24 will supply you with the zodiac sign the Moon occupied on the day of your birth. Look for your Moon Age Day down the left hand column and then for the letter you found in Stage 2. Where the two converge you will find a zodiac sign and this is the sign occupied by the Moon on the day that you were born.

Your Zodiac Moon Sign Explained

You will find a profile of all zodiac Moon Signs on pages 25 to 28, showing in yet another way how astrology helps to make you into the individual that you are. In each daily entry of the Astral Diary you can find the zodiac position of the Moon for every day of the year. This also allows you to discover your lunar birthdays. Since the Moon passes through all the signs of the zodiac in about a month, you can expect something like twelve lunar birthdays each year. At these times you are likely to be emotionally steady and able to make the sort of decisions that have real, lasting value.

MOON TABLE 1

YEAR	MAY	JUN	JUL	YEAR	MAY	JUN	JUL	YEAR	MAY	JUN	JUL
1914	24	23	22	1947	19	18	17	1980	14	13	12
1915	13	12	11	1948	9	7	6	1981	4	2	1/31
1916	2	1/30	30	1949	27	26	25	1982	21	21	20
1917	20	19	18	1950	17	15	15	1983	12	11	10
1918	10	8	8	1951	6	4	4	1984	1/30	29	28
1919	29	27	27	1952	23	22	22	1985	19	18	17
1920	18	16	15	1953	13	11	11	1986	8	7	7
1921	7	6	5	1954	2	1/30	29	1987	27	26	25
1922	26	25	24	1955	21	20	19	1988	15	14	13
1923	15	14	14	1956	10	8	8	1989	5	3	3
1924	3	2	2/31	1957	29	27	27	1990	24	22	22
1925	22	21	20	1958	18	17	16	1991	13	11	11
1926	11	10	9	1959	7	6	6	1992	2	1/30	29
1927	2/31	29	28	1960	26	24	24	1993	21	19	19
1928	19	18	17	1961	14	13	12	1994	10	8	8
1929	9	7	6	1962	4	2	1/31	1995	29	27	27
1930	28	26	25	1963	23	21	20	1996	18	17	15
1931	17	16	15	1964	11	10	9	1997	6	5	4
1932	5	4	3	1965	1/30	29	28	1998	25	24	23
1933	24	23	22	1966	19	18	17	1999	15	13	13
1934	13	12	11	1967	8	7	7	2000	4	2	1/31
1935	2	1/30	30	1968	27	26	25	2001	23	21	20
1936	20	19	18	1969	15	14	13	2002	12	10	9
1937	10	8	8	1970	6	4	4	2003	1/30	29	28
1938	29	27	27	1971	24	22	22	2004	18	16	16
1939	19	17	16	1972	13	11	11	2005	8	6	6
1940	7	6	5	1973	2	1/30	29	2006	27	26	25
1941	26	24	24	1974	21	20	19	2007	17	15	15
1942	15	13	13	1975	11	9	9	2008	5	4	3
1943	4	2	2	1976	29	27	27	2009	25	23	22
1944	22	20	20	1977	18	16	16	2010	14	12	12
1945	11	10	9	1978	7	5	5	2011	3	2	2
1946	1/30	29	28	1979	26	24	24	2012	20	19	19

TABLE 2

DAY	JUN	JUL
1	O	R
2	P	R
3	P	S
4	P	S
5	P	S
6	P	S
7	P	S
8	P	S
9	P	S
10	P	S
11	P	S
12	Q	S
13	Q	T
14	Q	T
15	Q	T
16	Q	T
17	Q	T
18	Q	T
19	Q	T
20	Q	T
21	Q	T
22	R	T
23	R	T
24	R	U
25	R	U
26	R	U
27	R	U
28	R	U
29	R	U
30	R	U
31	–	U

TABLE 3

M/D	O	P	Q	R	S	T	U
0	GE	GE	CA	CA	CA	LE	LE
1	GE	CA	CA	CA	LE	LE	LE
2	CA	CA	CA	LE	LE	LE	VI
3	CA	CA	LE	LE	LE	VI	VI
4	LE	LE	LE	LE	VI	VI	LI
5	LE	LE	VI	VI	VI	LI	LI
6	VI	VI	VI	VI	LI	LI	LI
7	VI	VI	LI	LI	LI	LI	SC
8	VI	VI	LI	LI	LI	SC	SC
9	LI	LI	SC	SC	SC	SC	SA
10	LI	LI	SC	SC	SC	SA	SA
11	SC	SC	SC	SA	SA	SA	CP
12	SC	SC	SA	SA	SA	SA	CP
13	SC	SA	SA	SA	SA	CP	CP
14	SA	SA	SA	CP	CP	CP	AQ
15	SA	SA	CP	CP	CP	AQ	AQ
16	CP	CP	CP	AQ	AQ	AQ	AQ
17	CP	CP	CP	AQ	AQ	AQ	PI
18	CP	CP	AQ	AQ	AQ	PI	PI
19	AQ	AQ	AQ	PI	PI	PI	PI
20	AQ	AQ	PI	PI	PI	AR	AR
21	AQ	PI	PI	PI	AR	AR	AR
22	PI	PI	PI	AR	AR	AR	TA
23	PI	PI	AR	AR	AR	TA	TA
24	PI	AR	AR	AR	TA	TA	TA
25	AR	AR	TA	TA	TA	GE	GE
26	AR	TA	TA	TA	GE	GE	GE
27	TA	TA	TA	GE	GE	GE	CA
28	TA	TA	GE	GE	GE	CA	CA
29	TA	GE	GE	GE	CA	CA	CA

AR = Aries, TA = Taurus, GE = Gemini, CA = Cancer, LE = Leo, VI = Virgo, LI = Libra, SC = Scorpio, SA = Sagittarius, CP = Capricorn, AQ = Aquarius, PI = Pisces

MOON SIGNS

Moon in Aries

You have a strong imagination, courage, determination and a desire to do things in your own way and forge your own path through life.

Originality is a key attribute; you are seldom stuck for ideas although your mind is changeable and you could take the time to focus on individual tasks. Often quick-tempered, you take orders from few people and live life at a fast pace. Avoid health problems by taking regular time out for rest and relaxation.

Emotionally, it is important that you talk to those you are closest to and work out your true feelings. Once you discover that people are there to help, there is less necessity for you to do everything yourself.

Moon in Taurus

The Moon in Taurus gives you a courteous and friendly manner, which means you are likely to have many friends.

The good things in life mean a lot to you, as Taurus is an Earth sign that delights in experiences which please the senses. Hence you are probably a lover of good food and drink, which may in turn mean you need to keep an eye on the bathroom scales, especially as looking good is also important to you.

Emotionally you are fairly stable and you stick by your own standards. Taureans do not respond well to change. Intuition also plays an important part in your life.

Moon in Gemini

You have a warm-hearted character, sympathetic and eager to help others. At times reserved, you can also be articulate and chatty: this is part of the paradox of Gemini, which always brings duplicity to the nature. You are interested in current affairs, have a good intellect, and are good company and likely to have many friends. Most of your friends have a high opinion of you and would be ready to defend you should the need arise. However, this is usually unnecessary, as you are quite capable of defending yourself in any verbal confrontation.

Travel is important to your inquisitive mind and you find intellectual stimulus in mixing with people from different cultures. You also gain much from reading, writing and the arts but you do need plenty of rest and relaxation in order to avoid fatigue.

Moon in Cancer

The Moon in Cancer at the time of birth is a fortunate position as Cancer is the Moon's natural home. This means that the qualities of compassion and understanding given by the Moon are especially enhanced in your nature, and you are friendly and sociable and cope well with emotional pressures. You cherish home and family life, and happily do the domestic tasks. Your surroundings are important to you and you hate squalor and filth. You are likely to have a love of music and poetry.

Your basic character, although at times changeable like the Moon itself, depends on symmetry. You aim to make your surroundings comfortable and harmonious, for yourself and those close to you.

Moon in Leo

The best qualities of the Moon and Leo come together to make you warmhearted, fair, ambitious and self-confident. With good organisational abilities, you invariably rise to a position of responsibility in your chosen career. This is fortunate as you don't enjoy being an 'also-ran' and would rather be an important part of a small organisation than a menial in a large one.

You should be lucky in love, and happy, provided you put in the effort to make a comfortable home for yourself and those close to you. It is likely that you will have a love of pleasure, sport, music and literature. Life brings you many rewards, most of them as a direct result of your own efforts, although you may be luckier than average and ready to make the best of any situation.

Moon in Virgo

You are endowed with good mental abilities and a keen receptive memory, but you are never ostentatious or pretentious. Naturally quite reserved, you still have many friends, especially of the opposite sex. Marital relationships must be discussed carefully and worked at so that they remain harmonious, as personal attachments can be a problem if you do not give them your full attention.

Talented and persevering, you possess artistic qualities and are a good homemaker. Earning your honours through genuine merit, you work long and hard towards your objectives but show little pride in your achievements. Many short journeys will be undertaken in your life.

Moon in Libra

With the Moon in Libra you are naturally popular and make friends easily. People like you, probably more than you realise, you bring fun to a party and are a natural diplomat. For all its good points, Libra is not the most stable of astrological signs and, as a result, your emotions can be a little unstable too. Therefore, although the Moon in Libra is said to be good for love and marriage, your Sun sign and Rising sign will have an important effect on your emotional and loving qualities.

You must remember to relate to others in your decision-making. Co-operation is crucial because Libra represents the 'balance' of life that can only be achieved through harmonious relationships. Conformity is not easy for you because Libra, an Air sign, likes its independence.

Moon in Scorpio

Some people might call you pushy. In fact, all you really want to do is to live life to the full and protect yourself and your family from the pressures of life. Take care to avoid giving the impression of being sarcastic or impulsive and use your energies wisely and constructively.

You have great courage and you invariably achieve your goals by force of personality and sheer effort. You are fond of mystery and are good at predicting the outcome of situations and events. Travel experiences can be beneficial to you.

You may experience problems if you do not take time to examine your motives in a relationship, and also if you allow jealousy, always a feature of Scorpio, to cloud your judgement.

Moon in Sagittarius

The Moon in Sagittarius helps to make you a generous individual with humanitarian qualities and a kind heart. Restlessness may be intrinsic as your mind is seldom still. Perhaps because of this, you have a need for change that could lead you to several major moves during your adult life. You are not afraid to stand your ground when you know your judgement is right, you speak directly and have good intuition.

At work you are quick, efficient and versatile and so you make an ideal employee. You need work to be intellectually demanding and do not enjoy tedious routines.

In relationships, you anger quickly if faced with stupidity or deception, though you are just as quick to forgive and forget. Emotionally, there are times when your heart rules your head.

Moon in Capricorn

The Moon in Capricorn makes you popular and likely to come into the public eye in some way. The watery Moon is not entirely comfortable in the Earth sign of Capricorn and this may lead to some difficulties in the early years of life. An initial lack of creative ability and indecision must be overcome before the true qualities of patience and perseverance inherent in Capricorn can show through.

You have good administrative ability and are a capable worker, and if you are careful you can accumulate wealth. But you must be cautious and take professional advice in partnerships, as you are open to deception. You may be interested in social or welfare work, which suit your organisational skills and sympathy for others.

Moon in Aquarius

The Moon in Aquarius makes you an active and agreeable person with a friendly, easy-going nature. Sympathetic to the needs of others, you flourish in a laid-back atmosphere. You are broad-minded, fair and open to suggestion, although sometimes you have an unconventional quality which others can find hard to understand.

You are interested in the strange and curious, and in old articles and places. You enjoy trips to these places and gain much from them. Political, scientific and educational work interests you and you might choose a career in science or technology.

Money-wise, you make gains through innovation and concentration and Lunar Aquarians often tackle more than one job at a time. In love you are kind and honest.

Moon in Pisces

You have a kind, sympathetic nature, somewhat retiring at times, but you always take account of others' feelings and help when you can.

Personal relationships may be problematic, but as life goes on you can learn from your experiences and develop a better understanding of yourself and the world around you.

You have a fondness for travel, appreciate beauty and harmony and hate disorder and strife. You may be fond of literature and would make a good writer or speaker yourself. You have a creative imagination and may come across as an incurable romantic. You have strong intuition, maybe bordering on a mediumistic quality, which sets you apart from the mass. You may not be rich in cash terms, but your personal gifts are worth more than gold.

CANCER IN LOVE

Discover how compatible you are with people from the same and other signs of the zodiac. Five stars equals a match made in heaven!

Cancer meets Cancer

This match will work because the couple share a mutual understanding. Cancerians are very kind people who also respond well to kindness from others, so a double Cancer match can almost turn into a mutual appreciation society! But this will not lead to selfish hedonism, as the Crab takes in order to give more. There is an impressive physical, emotional and spiritual meeting of minds, which will lead to a successful and inspiring pairing in its own low-key and deeply sensitive way. Star rating: *****

Cancer meets Leo

This relationship will usually be directed by Leo more towards its own needs than Cancer's. However, the Crab will willingly play second fiddle to more progressive and bossy types as it is deeply emotional and naturally supportive. Leo is bright, caring, magnanimous and protective and so, as long as it isn't over-assertive, this could be a good match. On the surface, Cancer appears the more conventional of the two, but Leo will discover, to its delight, that it can be unusual and quirky. Star rating: ****

Cancer meets Virgo

This match has little chance of success, for fairly simple reasons: Cancer's generous affection will be submerged by the Virgoan depths, not because Virgo is uncaring but because it expresses itself so differently. As both signs are naturally quiet, things might become a bit boring. They would be mutually supportive, possibly financially successful and have a very tidy house, but they won't share much sparkle, enthusiasm, risk-taking or passion. If this pair were stranded on a desert island, they might live at different ends of it. Star rating: **

Cancer meets Libra

Almost anyone can get on with Libra, which is one of the most adaptable signs of them all. But being adaptable does not always lead to fulfilment, and a successful match here will require a quiet Libran and a slightly more progressive Cancerian than the norm. Both signs are pleasant, polite and like domestic order, but Libra may find Cancer too emotional and perhaps lacking in vibrancy, while Libra, on the other hand, may be a little too flighty for steady Cancer. Star rating: ***

Cancer meets Scorpio

This match is potentially a great success, a fact which is often a mystery to astrologers. Some feel it is due to the compatibility of the Water element, but it could also come from a mixture of similarity and difference in the personalities. Scorpio is partly ruled by Mars, which gives it a deep, passionate, dominant and powerful side. Cancerians generally like and respect this amalgam, and recognise something there that they would like to adopt themselves. On the other side of the coin, Scorpio needs love and emotional security which Cancer offers generously. Star rating: *****

Cancer meets Sagittarius

Although probably not an immediate success, there is hope for this couple. It's hard to see how this pair could get together, because they have few mutual interests. Sagittarius is always on the go, loves a hectic social life and dances the night away. Cancer prefers the cinema or a concert. But, having met, Cancer will appreciate the Archer's happy and cheerful nature, while Sagittarius finds Cancer alluring and intriguing and, as the saying goes, opposites attract. A long-term relationship would focus on commitment to family, with Cancer leading this area. Star rating: ***

Cancer meets Capricorn

Just about the only thing this pair have in common is the fact that both signs begin with 'Ca'! Some signs of the zodiac are instigators and some are reactors, and both the Crab and the Goat are reactors. Consequently, they both need incentives from their partners but won't find it in each other and, with neither side taking the initiative, there's a spark missing. Cancer and Capricorn do think alike in some ways and so, if they can find their spark or common purpose, they can be as happy as anyone. It's just rather unlikely. Star rating: **

Cancer meets Aquarius

Cancer is often attracted to Aquarius and, as Aquarius is automatically on the side of anyone who fancies it, so there is the potential for something good here. Cancer loves Aquarius' devil-may-care approach to life, but also recognises and seeks to strengthen the basic lack of self-confidence that all Air signs try so hard to keep secret. Both signs are natural travellers and are quite adventurous. Their family life would be unusual, even peculiar, but friends would recognise a caring, sharing household with many different interests shared by people genuinely in love. Star rating: ***

Cancer meets Pisces

This is likely to be a very successful match. Cancer and Pisces are both Water signs, and are both deep, sensitive and very caring. Pisces loves deeply, and Cancer wants to be loved. There will be few fireworks here, and a very quiet house. But that doesn't mean that either love or action is lacking – the latter of which is just behind closed doors. Family and children are important to both signs and both are prepared to work hard, but Pisces is the more restless of the two and needs the support and security that Cancer offers. Star rating: *****

Cancer meets Aries

A potentially one-sided pairing, it often appears that the Cancerian is brow-beaten by the far more dominant Arian. So much depends on the patience of the Cancerian individual, because if good psychology is present – who knows? But beware, Aries, you may find your partner too passive, and constantly having to take the lead can be wearing – even for you. A prolonged trial period would be advantageous, as the match could easily go either way. When it does work, though, this relationship is usually contented. Star rating: ***

Cancer meets Taurus

This pair will have the tidiest house in the street – every stick of furniture in place, and no errant blade of grass daring to spoil the lawn. But things inside the relationship might not be quite so ship-shape as both signs need, but don't offer, encouragement. There's plenty of affection, but few incentives for mutual progress. This might not prevent material success, but an enduring relationship isn't based on money alone. Passion is essential, and both parties need to realise and aim for that.
Star rating: **

Cancer meets Gemini

This is often a very good match. Cancer is a very caring sign and quite adaptable. Geminis are untidy, have butterfly minds and are usually full of a thousand different schemes which Cancerians take in their stride and even relish. They can often be the 'wind beneath the wings' of their Gemini partners. In return, Gemini can eradicate some of the Cancerian emotional insecurity and will be more likely to be faithful in thought, word and deed to Cancer than to almost any other sign. Star rating: ****

VENUS:
THE PLANET OF LOVE

If you look up at the sky around sunset or sunrise you will often see Venus in close attendance to the Sun. It is arguably one of the most beautiful sights of all and there is little wonder that historically it became associated with the goddess of love. But although Venus does play an important part in the way you view love and in the way others see you romantically, this is only one of the spheres of influence that it enjoys in your overall character.

Venus has a part to play in the more cultured side of your life and has much to do with your appreciation of art, literature, music and general creativity. Even the way you look is responsive to the part of the zodiac that Venus occupied at the start of your life, though this fact is also down to your Sun sign and Ascending sign. If, at the time you were born, Venus occupied one of the more gregarious zodiac signs, you will be more likely to wear your heart on your sleeve, as well as to be more attracted to entertainment, social gatherings and good company. If on the other hand Venus occupied a quiet zodiac sign at the time of your birth, you would tend to be more retiring and less willing to shine in public situations.

It's good to know what part the planet Venus plays in your life for it can have a great bearing on the way you appear to the rest of the world and since we all have to mix with others, you can learn to make the very best of what Venus has to offer you.

One of the great complications in the past has always been trying to establish exactly what zodiac position Venus enjoyed when you were born because the planet is notoriously difficult to track. However, I have solved that problem by creating a table that is exclusive to your Sun sign, which you will find on the following page.

Establishing your Venus sign could not be easier. Just look up the year of your birth on the page opposite and you will see a sign of the zodiac. This was the sign that Venus occupied in the period covered by your sign in that year. If Venus occupied more than one sign during the period, this is indicated by the date on which the sign changed, and the name of the new sign. For instance, if you were born in 1950, Venus was in Taurus until the 27th June, after which time it was in Gemini. If you were born before 27th June your Venus sign is Taurus, if you were born on or after 27th June, your Venus sign is Gemini. Once you have established the position of Venus at the time of your birth, you can then look in the pages which follow to see how this has a bearing on your life as a whole.

1914 LEO / 16.7 VIRGO
1915 GEMINI / 11.7 CANCER
1916 CANCER
1917 CANCER / 5.7 LEO
1918 TAURUS / 29.6 GEMINI
1919 LEO / 8.7 VIRGO
1920 GEMINI / 25.6 CANCER /
18.7 LEO
1921 TAURUS / 8.7 GEMINI
1922 LEO / 15.7 VIRGO
1923 GEMINI / 10.7 CANCER
1924 CANCER
1925 CANCER / 4.7 LEO
1926 TAURUS / 28.6 GEMINI
1927 LEO / 8.7 VIRGO
1928 GEMINI / 24.6 CANCER /
18.7 LEO
1929 TAURUS / 8.7 GEMINI
1930 LEO / 15.7 VIRGO
1931 GEMINI / 10.7 CANCER
1932 CANCER
1933 CANCER / 4.7 LEO
1934 TAURUS / 27.6 GEMINI
1935 LEO / 8.7 VIRGO
1936 GEMINI / 24.6 CANCER /
17.7 LEO
1937 TAURUS / 8.7 GEMINI
1938 LEO / 14.7 VIRGO
1939 GEMINI / 9.7 CANCER
1940 CANCER / 13.7 GEMINI
1941 CANCER / 3.7 LEO
1942 TAURUS / 27.6 GEMINI
1943 LEO / 9.7 VIRGO
1944 GEMINI / 23.6 CANCER /
17.7 LEO
1945 TAURUS / 7.7 GEMINI
1946 LEO / 14.7 VIRGO
1947 GEMINI / 9.7 CANCER
1948 CANCER / 6.7 LEO
1949 CANCER / 2.7 LEO
1950 TAURUS / 27.6 GEMINI
1951 LEO / 9.7 VIRGO
1952 GEMINI / 23.6 CANCER /
17.7 LEO
1953 TAURUS / 7.7 GEMINI
1954 LEO / 13.7 VIRGO
1955 GEMINI / 8.7 CANCER
1956 CANCER / 29.6 GEMINI
1957 CANCER / 1.7 LEO
1958 TAURUS / 26.6 GEMINI
1959 LEO / 9.7 VIRGO
1960 CANCER / 16.7 LEO
1961 TAURUS / 7.7 GEMINI
1962 LEO / 13.7 VIRGO
1963 GEMINI / 8.7 CANCER

1964 CANCER / 22.6 GEMINI
1965 CANCER / 1.7 LEO
1966 TAURUS / 26.6 GEMINI
1967 LEO / 10.7 VIRGO
1968 CANCER / 16.7 LEO
1969 TAURUS / 6.7 GEMINI
1970 LEO / 13.7 VIRGO
1971 GEMINI / 7.7 CANCER
1972 CANCER / 22.6 GEMINI
1973 CANCER / 30.6 LEO
1974 TAURUS / 26.6 GEMINI /
22.7 CANCER
1975 LEO / 10.7 VIRGO
1976 CANCER / 15.7 LEO
1977 TAURUS / 6.7 GEMINI
1978 LEO / 12.7 VIRGO
1979 GEMINI / 7.7 CANCER
1980 CANCER / 22.6 GEMINI
1981 CANCER / 30.6 LEO
1982 TAURUS / 26.6 GEMINI /
21.7 CANCER
1983 LEO / 10.7 VIRGO
1984 CANCER / 15.7 LEO
1985 TAURUS / 6.7 GEMINI
1986 LEO / 12.7 VIRGO
1987 GEMINI / 6.7 CANCER
1988 CANCER / 22.6 GEMINI
1989 CANCER / 29.6 LEO
1990 TAURUS / 25.6 GEMINI /
20.7 CANCER
1991 LEO / 11.7 VIRGO
1992 CANCER / 14.7 LEO
1993 TAURUS / 5.7 GEMINI
1994 LEO / 11.7 VIRGO
1995 GEMINI / 5.7 CANCER
1996 CANCER / 22.6 GEMINI
1997 CANCER / 29.6 LEO
1998 TAURUS / 25.6 GEMINI /
20.7 CANCER
1999 LEO / 11.7 VIRGO
2000 CANCER / 14.7 LEO
2001 TAURUS / 5.7 GEMINI
2002 LEO / 11.7 VIRGO
2003 GEMINI / 5.7 CANCER
2004 CANCER / 22.6 GEMINI
2005 CANCER / 29.6 LEO
2006 TAURUS / 25.6 GEMINI /
20.7 CANCER
2007 LEO / 11.7 VIRGO
2008 CANCER / 14.7 LEO
2009 TAURUS / 5.7 GEMINI
2010 LEO / 11.7 VIRGO
2011 GEMINI / 5.7 CANCER
2012 CANCER / 22.6 GEMINI

VENUS THROUGH THE ZODIAC SIGNS

Venus in Aries

Amongst other things, the position of Venus in Aries indicates a fondness for travel, music and all creative pursuits. Your nature tends to be affectionate and you would try not to create confusion or difficulty for others if it could be avoided. Many people with this planetary position have a great love of the theatre, and mental stimulation is of the greatest importance. Early romantic attachments are common with Venus in Aries, so it is very important to establish a genuine sense of romantic continuity. Early marriage is not recommended, especially if it is based on sympathy. You may give your heart a little too readily on occasions.

Venus in Taurus

You are capable of very deep feelings and your emotions tend to last for a very long time. This makes you a trusting partner and lover, whose constancy is second to none. In life you are precise and careful and always try to do things the right way. Although this means an ordered life, which you are comfortable with, it can also lead you to be rather too fussy for your own good. Despite your pleasant nature, you are very fixed in your opinions and quite able to speak your mind. Others are attracted to you and historical astrologers always quoted this position of Venus as being very fortunate in terms of marriage. However, if you find yourself involved in a failed relationship, it could take you a long time to trust again.

Venus in Gemini

As with all associations related to Gemini, you tend to be quite versatile, anxious for change and intelligent in your dealings with the world at large. You may gain money from more than one source but you are equally good at spending it. There is an inference here that you are a good communicator, via either the written or the spoken word, and you love to be in the company of interesting people. Always on the look-out for culture, you may also be very fond of music, and love to indulge the curious and cultured side of your nature. In romance you tend to have more than one relationship and could find yourself associated with someone who has previously been a friend or even a distant relative.

Venus in Cancer

You often stay close to home because you are very fond of family and enjoy many of your most treasured moments when you are with those you love. Being naturally sympathetic, you will always do anything you can to support those around you, even people you hardly know at all. This charitable side of your nature is your most noticeable trait and is one of the reasons why others are naturally so fond of you. Being receptive and in some cases even psychic, you can see through to the soul of most of those with whom you come into contact. You may not commence too many romantic attachments but when you do give your heart, it tends to be unconditionally.

Venus in Leo

It must become quickly obvious to almost anyone you meet that you are kind, sympathetic and yet determined enough to stand up for anyone or anything that is truly important to you. Bright and sunny, you warm the world with your natural enthusiasm and would rarely do anything to hurt those around you, or at least not intentionally. In romance you are ardent and sincere, though some may find your style just a little overpowering. Gains come through your contacts with other people and this could be especially true with regard to romance, for love and money often come hand in hand for those who were born with Venus in Leo. People claim to understand you, though you are more complex than you seem.

Venus in Virgo

Your nature could well be fairly quiet no matter what your Sun sign might be, though this fact often manifests itself as an inner peace and would not prevent you from being basically sociable. Some delays and even the odd disappointment in love cannot be ruled out with this planetary position, though it's a fact that you will usually find the happiness you look for in the end. Catapulting yourself into romantic entanglements that you know to be rather ill-advised is not sensible, and it would be better to wait before you committed yourself exclusively to any one person. It is the essence of your nature to serve the world at large and through doing so it is possible that you will attract money at some stage in your life.

Venus in Libra

Venus is very comfortable in Libra and bestows upon those people who have this planetary position a particular sort of kindness that is easy to recognise. This is a very good position for all sorts of friendships and also for romantic attachments that usually bring much joy into your life. Few individuals with Venus in Libra would avoid marriage and since you are capable of great depths of love, it is likely that you will find a contented personal life. You like to mix with people of integrity and intelligence but don't take kindly to scruffy surroundings or work that means getting your hands too dirty. Careful speculation, good business dealings and money through marriage all seem fairly likely.

Venus in Scorpio

You are quite open and tend to spend money quite freely, even on those occasions when you don't have very much. Although your intentions are always good, there are times when you get yourself in to the odd scrape and this can be particularly true when it comes to romance, which you may come to late or from a rather unexpected direction. Certainly you have the power to be happy and to make others contented on the way, but you find the odd stumbling block on your journey through life and it could seem that you have to work harder than those around you. As a result of this, you gain a much deeper understanding of the true value of personal happiness than many people ever do, and are likely to achieve true contentment in the end.

Venus in Sagittarius

You are lighthearted, cheerful and always able to see the funny side of any situation. These facts enhance your popularity, which is especially high with members of the opposite sex. You should never have to look too far to find romantic interest in your life, though it is just possible that you might be too willing to commit yourself before you are certain that the person in question is right for you. Part of the problem here extends to other areas of life too. The fact is that you like variety in everything and so can tire of situations that fail to offer it. All the same, if you choose wisely and learn to understand your restless side, then great happiness can be yours.

Venus in Capricorn

The most notable trait that comes from Venus in this position is that it makes you trustworthy and able to take on all sorts of responsibilities in life. People are instinctively fond of you and love you all the more because you are always ready to help those who are in any form of need. Social and business popularity can be yours and there is a magnetic quality to your nature that is particularly attractive in a romantic sense. Anyone who wants a partner for a lover, a spouse and a good friend too would almost certainly look in your direction. Constancy is the hallmark of your nature and unfaithfulness would go right against the grain. You might sometimes be a little too trusting.

Venus in Aquarius

This location of Venus offers a fondness for travel and a desire to try out something new at every possible opportunity. You are extremely easy to get along with and tend to have many friends from varied backgrounds, classes and inclinations. You like to live a distinct sort of life and gain a great deal from moving about, both in a career sense and with regard to your home. It is not out of the question that you could form a romantic attachment to someone who comes from far away or be attracted to a person of a distinctly artistic and original nature. What you cannot stand is jealousy, for you have friends of both sexes and would want to keep things that way.

Venus in Pisces

The first thing people tend to notice about you is your wonderful, warm smile. Being very charitable by nature you will do anything to help others, even if you don't know them well. Much of your life may be spent sorting out situations for other people, but it is very important to feel that you are living for yourself too. In the main, you remain cheerful, and tend to be quite attractive to members of the opposite sex. Where romantic attachments are concerned, you could be drawn to people who are significantly older or younger than yourself or to someone with a unique career or point of view. It might be best for you to avoid marrying whilst you are still very young.

THE ASTRAL DIARY
HOW THE DIAGRAMS WORK

Through the picture diagrams in the Astral Diary I want to help you to plot your year. With them you can see where the positive and negative aspects will be found in each month. To make the most of them, all you have to do is remember where and when!

Let me show you how they work ...

THE MONTH AT A GLANCE

Just as there are twelve separate zodiac signs, so astrologers believe that each sign has twelve separate aspects to life. Each of the twelve segments relates to a different personal aspect. I list them all every month so that their meanings are always clear.

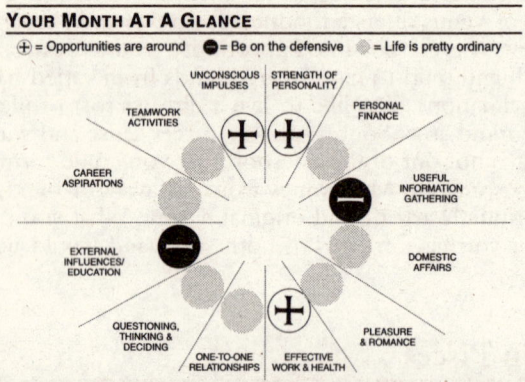

YOUR MONTH AT A GLANCE

⊕ = Opportunities are around ⊖ = Be on the defensive ◯ = Life is pretty ordinary

UNCONSCIOUS IMPULSES
STRENGTH OF PERSONALITY
TEAMWORK ACTIVITIES
PERSONAL FINANCE
CAREER ASPIRATIONS
USEFUL INFORMATION GATHERING
EXTERNAL INFLUENCES/ EDUCATION
DOMESTIC AFFAIRS
QUESTIONING, THINKING & DECIDING
PLEASURE & ROMANCE
ONE-TO-ONE RELATIONSHIPS
EFFECTIVE WORK & HEALTH

I have designed this chart to show you how and when these twelve different aspects are being influenced throughout the year. When there is a shaded circle, nothing out of the ordinary is to be expected. However, when a circle turns white with a plus sign, the influence is positive. Where the circle is black with a minus sign, it is a negative.

YOUR ENERGY RHYTHM CHART

On the opposite page is a picture diagram in which I link your zodiac group to the rhythm of the Moon. In doing this I have calculated when you will be gaining strength from its influence and equally when you may be weakened by it.

If you think of yourself as being like the tides of the ocean then you may understand how your own energies must also rise and fall. And if you understand how it works and when it is working, then you can better organise your activities to achieve more and get things done more easily.

YOUR ENERGY RHYTHM CHART
At your best on 20th–21st

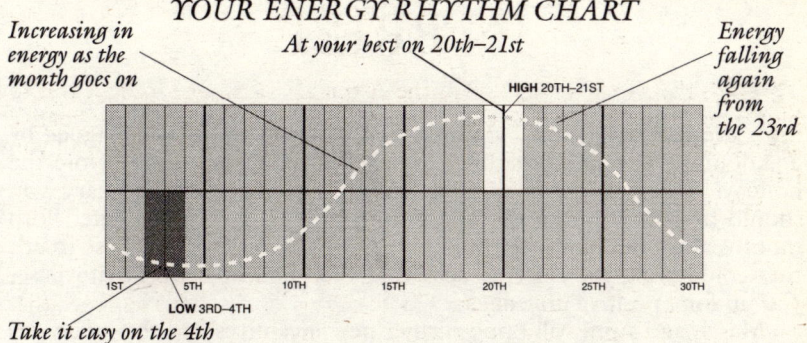

Increasing in energy as the month goes on

HIGH 20TH–21ST

Energy falling again from the 23rd

1ST 5TH 10TH 15TH 20TH 25TH 30TH

LOW 3RD–4TH

Take it easy on the 4th

MOVING PICTURE SCREEN
Love, money, career and vitality measured every week

The diagram at the end of each week is designed to be informative and fun. The arrows move up and down the scale to give you an idea of the strength of your opportunities in each area. If LOVE stands at plus 4, then get out and put yourself about because things are going your way in romance! The further down the arrow goes, the weaker the opportunities. Do note that the diagram is an overall view of your astrological aspects and therefore reflects a trend which may not concur with every day in that cycle.

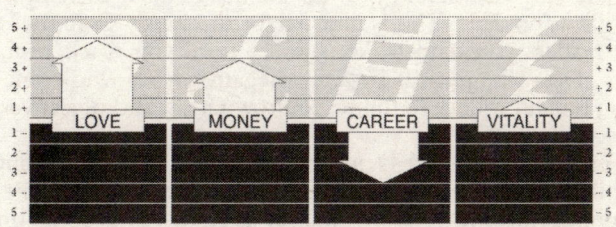

5 +				+ 5
4 +				+ 4
3 +				+ 3
2 +				+ 2
1 +				+ 1
1 –	LOVE	MONEY	CAREER	VITALITY	1
2 –				2
3 –				3
4 –				4
5 –				5

AND FINALLY:

am...

pm ....

The two lines that are left blank in each daily entry of the Astral Diary are for your own personal use. You may find them ideal for keeping a check on birthdays or appointments, though it could also be an idea to make notes from the astrological trends and diagrams a few weeks in advance. Some of the lines are marked with a key, which indicates the working of astrological cycles in your life. Look out for them each week as they are the best days to take action or make decisions. The daily text tells you which area of your life to focus on.

☿ = Mercury is retrograde on that day.

CANCER: YOUR YEAR IN BRIEF

As the year gets started you may find that you are feeling plagued by doubts, especially regarding things you didn't get done before the holidays. Don't worry because in January, and especially February, you should be able to grasp the opportunity to get right up to date. Both months also offer new incentives, and if you respond well to these trends they could bring you closer to achieving a few new objectives that will set you up for a positive time ahead.

March and April will bring further new incentives and the influences are especially good when it comes to achieving your heart's desire in a romantic sense. You will be in a good position to make overtures to others at this time. These should be well received, and there is little doubt that you have an ability to break through red tape and to get where you want to be. Take special care of friends at this time.

The early summer may turn out to be just about the best time for you. Chances are you will be feeling less constrained and it would be no bad thing to use those chances to spread your wings, especially in terms of travel. There are some small but significant financial gains to be made during May and June, and many Cancerians could be thinking about changes to career structures as this part of the year arrives.

July and August will find you still anxious to make as many alterations to your life as possible. This is unusual for the steady Crab, but once you become restless you tend to keep going until you reach your ultimate objective. Don't be put off by a few negative types who come along at this time; remain willing to follow your own ideas and objectives through both months.

During September and October you should be more willing to stop for a while and to watch what is going on around you. It isn't that you have stopped moving forward, merely that this is a good time to be consolidating your position in life. You may be offering a great deal of help to others at this stage and you come across as being particularly selfless. People always love you but are likely to be even more warm to you at this stage of the year.

The last two months of the year look like a less active and enterprising phase. If you are somewhat unwilling to go that extra mile, as you did in the summer, you may need to draw on your will power a little more. A more conservative attitude is possible, especially in November, and consolidation is the key. By the Christmas period you will be gaining speed again and, as is usually the case for you, putting yourself out so that others can enjoy themselves.

January

2012

YOUR MONTH AT A GLANCE

⊕ = Opportunities are around   ⊖ = Be on the defensive   ⬤ = Life is pretty ordinary

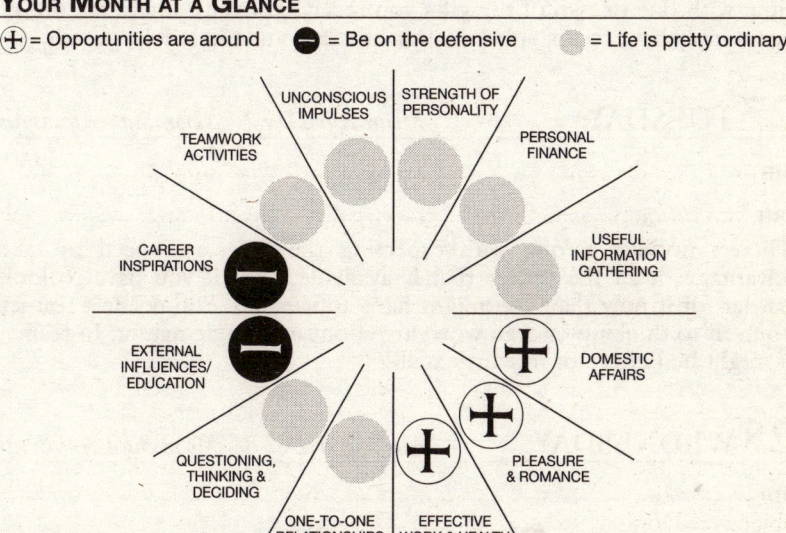

- UNCONSCIOUS IMPULSES
- STRENGTH OF PERSONALITY
- TEAMWORK ACTIVITIES
- PERSONAL FINANCE
- CAREER INSPIRATIONS
- USEFUL INFORMATION GATHERING
- EXTERNAL INFLUENCES/ EDUCATION
- DOMESTIC AFFAIRS
- QUESTIONING, THINKING & DECIDING
- PLEASURE & ROMANCE
- ONE-TO-ONE RELATIONSHIPS
- EFFECTIVE WORK & HEALTH

JANUARY HIGHS AND LOWS

Here I show you how the rhythms of the Moon will affect you this month. Like the tide, your energies and abilities will rise and fall with its pattern. When it is above the centre line, go for it, when it is below, you should be resting.

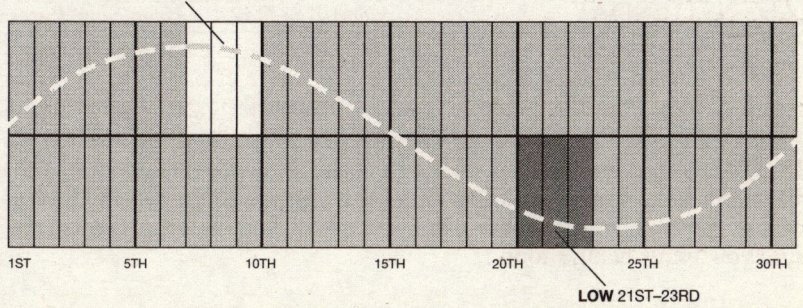

HIGH 8TH–10TH

1ST   5TH   10TH   15TH   20TH   25TH   30TH

LOW 21ST–23RD

41

26 MONDAY
Moon Age Day 1   Moon Sign Capricorn

am ....

pm...

The lunar low is still around for Boxing Day, so you may decide to keep things even quieter than yesterday. Today lends itself to putting your feet up and watching an old movie on television, or maybe spending some time with one or two of the gifts you received. Even if there are things you simply have to do, you can afford to save some time for yourself.

27 TUESDAY
Moon Age Day 2   Moon Sign Aquarius

am ....

pm...

There's nothing wrong with expecting the best. You need to take advantage of all the variety that is available, even if you have to look harder for it now than you might have anticipated. You needn't restrict yourself to thinking or even worrying about one single matter. In reality, it might be better not to worry at all!

28 WEDNESDAY
Moon Age Day 3   Moon Sign Aquarius

am ....

pm...

A continuing and increased boost to relationships means that you can gain much in the way of rewards. Personal attachment is the area of life that serves you best and the one on which you are encouraged to concentrate at present. Your diplomatic skills are emphasised, and could come in handy at some stage later in the day, particularly in family settings.

29 THURSDAY
Moon Age Day 4   Moon Sign Pisces

am ....

pm...

Broadening your horizons is very important now, ahead of the New Year. It's time to show your strong sense of culture and your refined taste. You shouldn't be too quick to judge either the attitude or the sensibilities of others. All in all, you can make this a very useful day – as long as you make sure you aren't being snooty!

30 FRIDAY
Moon Age Day 5   Moon Sign Pisces

am ....

pm..

By all means enjoy the family side of the Christmas holidays, though planetary trends just now also favour romantic twosomes. This has potential to be a generally happy day and one that allows you to reach a better understanding of the way someone close to you actually ticks. The key is to listen rather than talk right now.

31 SATURDAY
Moon Age Day 6   Moon Sign Pisces

am ....

pm..

If there are a range of celebrations taking place around you today, it might be difficult to decide what you actually want to do. Spreading yourself around is one option, but it isn't without problems. It might be best to just toss a coin and make the most of whatever fate offers. Your determination to have a really good evening is what really counts.

1 SUNDAY
Moon Age Day 7   Moon Sign Aries

am ....

pm..

It's a great start to the year as far as you are concerned. With everything to play for in a practical sense it looks as though some of the ideas you have delayed during the holidays can now be put into practice immediately. There should be help from family members and a great deal of popularity with people who really matter.

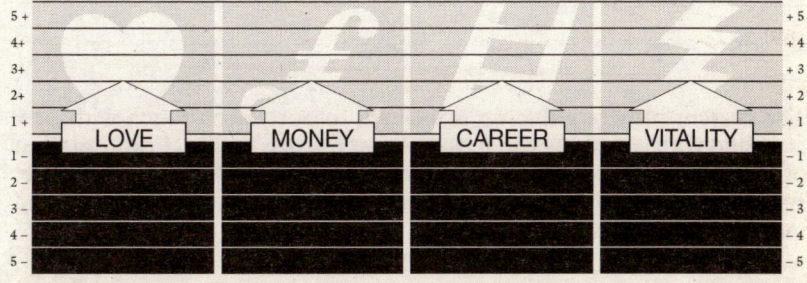

2 MONDAY
Moon Age Day 8   Moon Sign Aries

am ....

pm...

You can easily impress others in most areas of your life today. Unfortunately, you may get mixed reactions when other people realise that you cannot back everyone's point of view. But you cannot rely simply on diplomacy. The time has come to answer truthfully any question you are asked and to lay all your cards on the table.

3 TUESDAY
Moon Age Day 9   Moon Sign Taurus

am ....

pm...

With many practical situations around at the moment you will want to take full advantage of them all. You can get things done at home and seem to have a particularly good ability to organise and arrange things. All in all, this will turn out to be a busy day, and one during which you should be working to your full potential.

4 WEDNESDAY
Moon Age Day 10   Moon Sign Taurus

am ....

pm...

You should find this to be a good period for personal and communication matters. You have the odd trick or two up your sleeve and can use them to get ahead of the herd. This is an excellent time for all sporting activities or for deciding to take a spontaneous journey. This is a confident time for you so use it!

5 THURSDAY
Moon Age Day 11   Moon Sign Taurus

am ....

pm...

The present planetary line-up is inclined to put you in touch with new faces and with situations you have not come across before. Confrontation of any sort needs to be avoided at present, in favour of a harmonious life. Excitement is possible in the evening but only if you get out there and make it happen.

6 FRIDAY   *Moon Age Day 12   Moon Sign Gemini*

am ....

pm...

It's likely that today will turn out to be a time when you choose to please yourself. Try to avoid getting too tied up with domestic issues, most of which will sort themselves out if you give them time. Instead, do something that you really find interesting and be with people whose presence makes you happy.

7 SATURDAY   *Moon Age Day 13   Moon Sign Gemini*

am ....

pm...

The pace of everyday life is increasing dramatically so make sure you are not left out in the cold when there are gains to be made. All the same, this is a day for planning, rather than one for specifically doing. Tomorrow comes soon enough, when the Moon enters your zodiac sign. For the moment, look ahead.

8 SUNDAY   *Moon Age Day 14   Moon Sign Cancer*

am ....

pm...

The Moon enters your zodiac sign, bringing one of the most productive and generally lucky periods of the month and the time known as the lunar high. Whatever you take on today, go for gold. Don't be shy of letting people know you are around and show even those who think they know you that there is more to you than meets the eye.

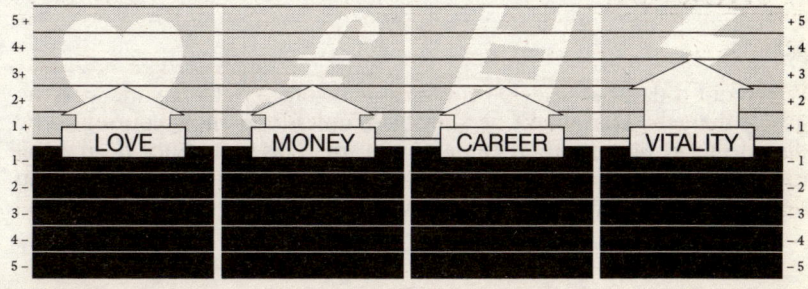

9 MONDAY
Moon Age Day 15   Moon Sign Cancer

am ....

pm...

You won't be fazed by the fact that you are likely to be busy today. You should be at your best if you get out and about and certainly would not take kindly to being cooped up in the same place all day. Lady Luck is on your side so look out for a few surprises by the latter part of the day.

10 TUESDAY
Moon Age Day 16   Moon Sign Cancer

am ....

pm...

The period of optimism and vitality continues. For most of today, you should be taking advantage of the excellent prospects for getting on in life around at the moment. Don't be in the least surprised if you discover that people are paying you extraordinary compliments. The fact is that you are much loved, and it shows at present.

11 WEDNESDAY
Moon Age Day 17   Moon Sign Leo

am ....

pm...

Things are looking exciting for the Crab and you may feel the need to broaden your horizons, which could include taking the opportunity to travel more this year. The chance to begin planning a trip begins almost immediately, so grab it with both hands. Take a broad view of any potential opportunities, particularly for yourself.

12 THURSDAY
Moon Age Day 18   Moon Sign Leo

am ....

pm...

Watch out today, because you could easily be taken in by anyone with the gift of the gab. That won't be a problem unless you allow yourself to be duped simply because they spin a good yarn. This would not be an ideal day for making major purchases or for doing anything that relies on snap decisions rather than rational thought.

13 FRIDAY
Moon Age Day 19   Moon Sign Virgo

am ....

pm..

It looks as though your competitive instincts will be promoted today and you should be making it very clear that you know what you want from life and how to go about getting it. Social impulses are very strong so you should not be hesitant when it comes to mixing and mingling with a whole variety of different people.

14 SATURDAY
Moon Age Day 20   Moon Sign Virgo

am ....

pm..

Look out today because there could be a few disputes, either in your working life or socially. If this turns out to be the case, it might be best to withdraw from situations you recognise as being awkward. You don't care to cause problems and might prefer to spend some time on your own rather than contributing to discord.

15 SUNDAY
Moon Age Day 21   Moon Sign Libra

am ....

pm..

Social trends are now looking a good deal better and you will be getting on extremely well with almost everyone. Of course family members and friends come first in your life, but if you find time for people you don't know so well, you will enjoy a hectic personal schedule at this time. One or two journeys are highly likely.

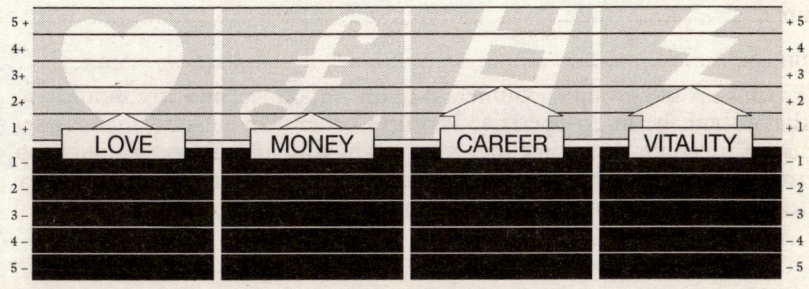

16 MONDAY
Moon Age Day 22   Moon Sign Libra

am ....

pm...

At the start of this week you are more than usually willing to fall in line with the opinions of people you trust, and you might even be listening to what strangers have to say. Your kind disposition finds you willing to help almost anyone who is having problems. This is no surprise because it's a big part of the way you always are.

17 TUESDAY
Moon Age Day 23   Moon Sign Scorpio

am ....

pm...

The pace of your everyday life is increasing, so you should be open to all sorts of new incentives and be planning into them carefully. One crucial factor is that you should not exhaust yourself because then you will achieve very little. Family members take on a special importance for you.

18 WEDNESDAY
Moon Age Day 24   Moon Sign Scorpio

am ....

pm...

Don't be surprised if discussions and negotiations about what you see as vital issues do not strike others in quite the same way. You will need to remain patient and should not allow the more brooding side of your Cancer nature to get in the way of thinking objectively. Perhaps you need to explain yourself better.

19 THURSDAY
Moon Age Day 25   Moon Sign Sagittarius

am ....

pm...

Friendship and group encounters take on a good feel and you should use that to engage in co-operative ventures of any kind. Good friends you haven't seen for some time may reappear in your life and you should keep an ear open for general gossip that might be of interest. Plan a journey today, even if it won't take place for months.

20 FRIDAY — *Moon Age Day 26   Moon Sign Sagittarius*

am ....

pm...

In some respects you want everything you can get from life and if you go for it, you can have it now. The world looks good from the Crab's perspective at this time and you should be making sure you get on well with practical projects. Cancerians working under these positive influences are a force to be reckoned with.

21 SATURDAY — *Moon Age Day 27   Moon Sign Capricorn*

am ....

pm...

The Moon is in your opposite sign and there are disruptive influences about, thanks to the presence of the lunar low, but be reassured that these are hardly likely to have a bearing on your life in anything but a temporary way. It would be good to spend time on your own today, doing something you really enjoy without interference.

22 SUNDAY — *Moon Age Day 28   Moon Sign Capricorn*

am ....

pm...

A lull is in place and there doesn't seem to be a great deal you can do about it. Settle for quiet pursuits and spend time with family members. As long as you are not champing at the bit to get on with jobs that simply can't be done, there is no reason to view this as a particularly unlucky or difficult day.

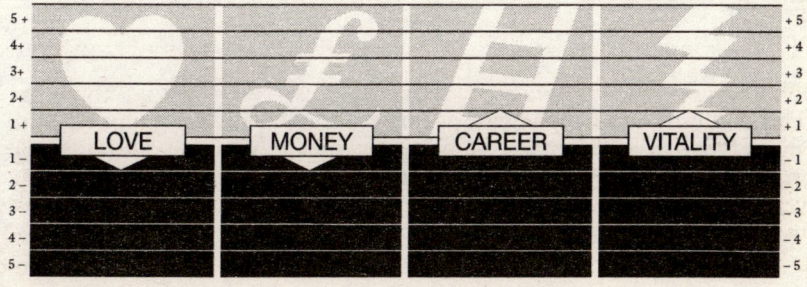

23 MONDAY
Moon Age Day 0   Moon Sign Capricorn

am ....

pm..

The slow patch is still in operation. Getting things moving won't be easy, so leave it for today and make ready to push forward again tomorrow. For the moment watch, wait and listen. Something that a friend is saying could be of particular importance and even though you don't react much now, you should be paying attention.

24 TUESDAY
Moon Age Day 1   Moon Sign Aquarius

am ....

pm..

There are a few issues at work that might seem to be more trouble than they are worth now. That means leaving them alone and certainly does not indicate a period during which you should blow them up out of all proportion. With plenty to play for in the relationship stakes, don't be too embarrassed to tell people how you feel.

25 WEDNESDAY
Moon Age Day 2   Moon Sign Aquarius

am ....

pm..

It's clear you are busy at the moment but that need not prevent you from taking on even more. You tend to be in the mood to count your blessings and that means you remain generally cheerful, even on the odd occasion when things go wrong. Your patience over a particular issue will be rewarded soon.

26 THURSDAY
Moon Age Day 3   Moon Sign Pisces

am ....

pm..

This ought to be a happy phase at home, though with less going for it in an everyday sense. To make the best of it, stick to what you know as you may not feel comfortable when facing situations you don't understand very well. Comfort and security seem to mean a great deal to you as the weekend approaches.

27 FRIDAY
Moon Age Day 4   Moon Sign Pisces

am ....

pm...

The things you hear from others today can easily contribute to your fund of knowledge, so don't hold back when it comes to listening in. If you are accused of being nosy, you will simply have to shrug your shoulders because basically it's true at the moment. However, the rewards for paying attention can be great.

28 SATURDAY
Moon Age Day 5   Moon Sign Aries

am ....

pm...

Saturday should bring a definite boost to your social life and you should be confident enough to mix more freely with the sort of people you may sometimes avoid. Romance is on the cards for the young or young at heart Cancerians, with compliments coming to all Crabs, sometimes from unexpected directions.

29 SUNDAY
Moon Age Day 6   Moon Sign Aries

am ....

pm...

Fairly untypically for Cancer, you could be feeling more determined than ever to get your own way. That doesn't mean you are forgetting about the needs of others. On the contrary, for every success you make, there are plenty of other people feeling the benefits too. Lady Luck is on your side and you need to give her all the help you can.

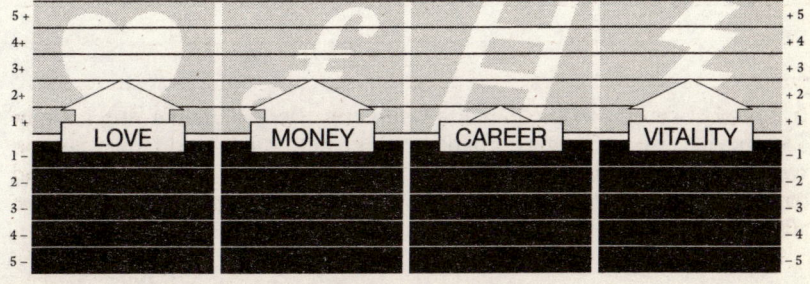

30 MONDAY
Moon Age Day 7   Moon Sign Aries

am ....

pm...

There ought to be plenty of time for fun and games, some of a deeply personal nature. A winter holiday would suit you down to the ground at this time but if you can't get one, you could at least arrange to spend a day away from everyday routines. It might be a good day to see if you can find a bargain in the January sales.

31 TUESDAY
Moon Age Day 8   Moon Sign Taurus

am ....

pm...

There is a slight possibility that strong disagreements may crop up today. Such a state of affairs will only happen if those around you insist on being right all the time. For your own part, watch out because the position of Mars in your chart at present can make you stubborn and unwilling to admit that you might just be wrong about something.

1 WEDNESDAY
Moon Age Day 9   Moon Sign Taurus

am ....

pm...

With a new month comes a slight change in attitude regarding issues you thought you understood only too well. By nature, you are quite capable of being adaptable and that is very important at this time. Get on with necessary tasks today but keep one eye on events that are unfolding around you and be willing to make changes as a result.

2 THURSDAY
Moon Age Day 10   Moon Sign Gemini

am ....

pm...

It is almost certain that you will be thinking about personal issues today and maybe also seeking to change the ground rules with regards to a relationship. People you haven't seen for some time could be coming back into your life soon, bringing with them some surprising news. Look after the pennies when it comes to purchases.

3 FRIDAY   *Moon Age Day 11   Moon Sign Gemini*

am ....

pm...

Love beckons and the chance of potential romantic highlights is very strong at the moment, particularly for young or single Cancerians. It is likely that someone has had their eye on you for a while and is only now plucking up the courage to say so. Even long-term relationships look more exciting under present astrological trends.

4 SATURDAY   *Moon Age Day 12   Moon Sign Gemini*

am ....

pm...

This Saturday should mark a positive period on the domestic scene. It looks as though you are in for some interesting times with regard to family members, with younger people figuring strongly. Although you won't consider yourself to be particularly lucky at the moment, there are some gains possible.

5 SUNDAY   *Moon Age Day 13   Moon Sign Cancer*

am ....

pm...

The Moon returns to your zodiac sign, offering a splendid day with plenty to set it apart and no lack of attention coming your way. Now is perhaps the time to take a small chance financially because good luck is likely to be with you. Conforming to expectations might be hard but you can get away with it now.

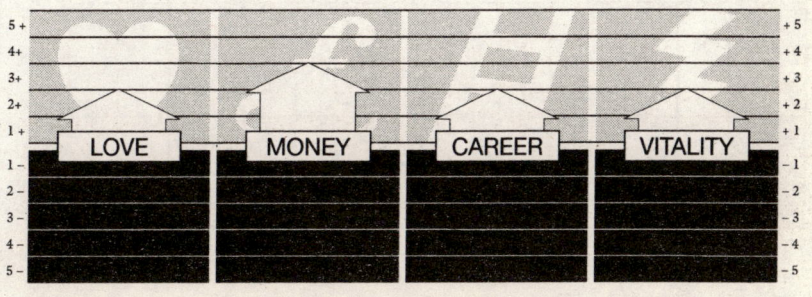

February
2012

YOUR MONTH AT A GLANCE

+ = Opportunities are around   − = Be on the defensive   ● = Life is pretty ordinary

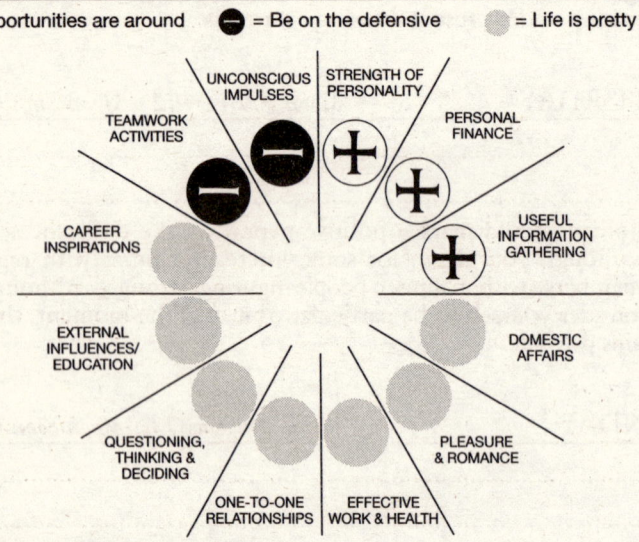

- UNCONSCIOUS IMPULSES
- STRENGTH OF PERSONALITY
- TEAMWORK ACTIVITIES
- PERSONAL FINANCE
- CAREER INSPIRATIONS
- USEFUL INFORMATION GATHERING
- EXTERNAL INFLUENCES/ EDUCATION
- DOMESTIC AFFAIRS
- QUESTIONING, THINKING & DECIDING
- PLEASURE & ROMANCE
- ONE-TO-ONE RELATIONSHIPS
- EFFECTIVE WORK & HEALTH

FEBRUARY HIGHS AND LOWS

Here I show you how the rhythms of the Moon will affect you this month. Like the tide, your energies and abilities will rise and fall with its pattern. When it is above the centre line, go for it, when it is below, you should be resting.

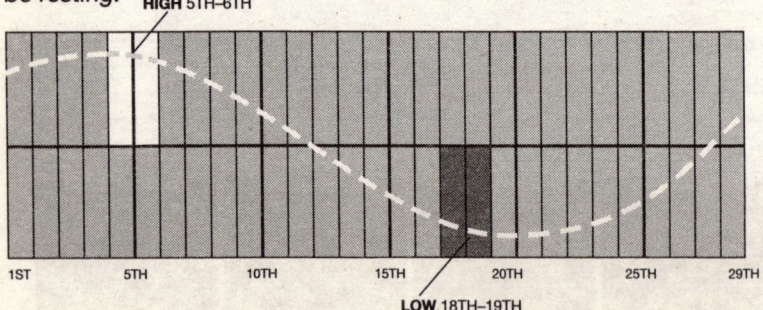

HIGH 5TH–6TH

1ST   5TH   10TH   15TH   20TH   25TH   29TH

LOW 18TH–19TH

6 MONDAY
Moon Age Day 14   Moon Sign Cancer

am ....

pm...

It ought to be possible for you to coast towards your chosen destination today. You have more than a modicum of good luck on your side and in any case you can demonstrate considerable technical skill in the way you are doing things. Although you are not exactly rushing your fences right now, you can still come out ahead.

7 TUESDAY
Moon Age Day 15   Moon Sign Leo

am ....

pm...

Positive trends strengthen and today you simply have to be the centre of attention. It isn't something you set out to do, but merely a consequence of the way you are functioning at present. Get yourself into the good books of someone who has influence at work. This is the month of possible advancement.

8 WEDNESDAY
Moon Age Day 16   Moon Sign Leo

am ....

pm...

Anything that takes you out of yourself and feeds your imagination has got to be good today. However, you won't be in the market for anything smutty or seedy right now. Others may balk at that fact but that's just the way you are. There is room in everyone's life for intellectual improvements, even that of the cultured Crab.

9 THURSDAY
Moon Age Day 17   Moon Sign Virgo

am ....

pm...

Keep moving forward. There is very little to hold you back now, particularly since you have been taking measures in the recent past to get what you want from life, while still taking the needs of others in your life into consideration. Romance is on the cards for Cancer at this time. If you have been looking for love, intensify your search today.

10 FRIDAY
Moon Age Day 18   Moon Sign Virgo

am ....

pm..

You should be happiest when you are with close friends today, as this will avoid the slight loss of confidence you may have been experiencing in public settings. What does remain absolutely intact is your sense of humour, though, so use it to good advantage to see you through a potentially embarrassing situation.

11 SATURDAY
Moon Age Day 19   Moon Sign Libra

am ....

pm..

On the ideas front, you might discover that you are more sluggish than was the case a week or two ago. Be willing to think things through carefully and avoid rushing at projects. You may find that a little jealousy crops up today, but don't allow that little green-eyed monster to possess you.

12 SUNDAY
Moon Age Day 20   Moon Sign Libra

am ....

pm..

It will be prudent to pay attention to things around you today. There is a good deal of useful input coming your way and it appears that you have all it takes to make ground over competitors. Fate offers some significant opportunities, so do make sure you keep your eyes open and be ready to take advantage of those that arise.

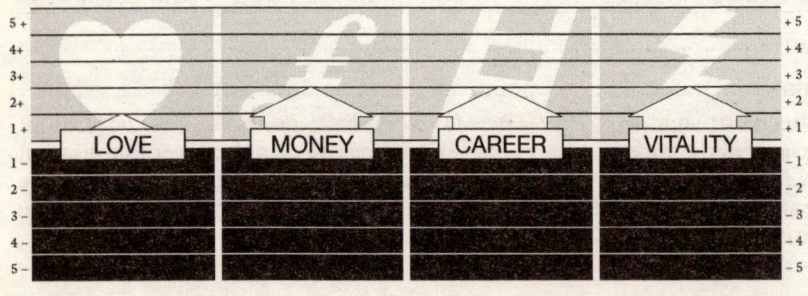

13 MONDAY
Moon Age Day 21   Moon Sign Scorpio

am ....

pm...

It is towards family matters that you now turn. There could be small disputes in relationships, but none of them is even necessary if you think carefully first. Don't put off until tomorrow any task you can reasonably do today and make sure you are out of bed early in the day. You may not like the prospect, but you will be glad later.

14 TUESDAY
Moon Age Day 22   Moon Sign Scorpio

am ....

pm...

Venus in particular is shining on you so leisure and pleasure pursuits should now be more rewarding than ever. Although you are apt to be very busy during the day, the most enjoyable period is likely to be in the evening. Romance is around, particularly for young Cancerians or those who have been actively looking for love.

15 WEDNESDAY
Moon Age Day 23   Moon Sign Scorpio

am ....

pm...

The stars seem to be shining on you. This ought to be one of the better days of the month to achieve what you want from life generally. You are not in an argumentative frame of mind so shouldn't feel the need to rise to any bait that is offered. Artistic pursuits could capture your imagination, especially in any home-based projects.

16 THURSDAY
Moon Age Day 24   Moon Sign Sagittarius

am ....

pm...

Thanks to Mercury, sociable trends are on the increase and communication comes to the fore. You seem ready to talk to just about anyone and should accept any social invitations that come your way, especially if they put you in the spotlight in some way. You may be less enthusiastic about any romantic overtures aimed at you.

17 FRIDAY

Moon Age Day 25   Moon Sign Sagittarius

am..

pm..

You could strengthen your finances today if you take action to consolidate a position you chose recently. In addition, you may find that decisions you took some weeks or months ago are now beginning to pay dividends. Friends could be especially reliant on you at present and you will need to find the time to show them your support.

18 SATURDAY

Moon Age Day 26   Moon Sign Capricorn

am..

pm..

Put a brake on your ambitions for the next two days as the lunar low is going to slow you down in any case and there is really no point in fighting against the odds. Instead, do what you can to relax and enjoy yourself, then be ready to get back to normal when the planetary influences improve.

19 SUNDAY

Moon Age Day 27   Moon Sign Capricorn

am..

pm..

You tend to be quieter than of late and could be inclined to play your cards too close to your chest. Confirming your strengths will have to wait because you could be too preoccupied with your failings. As long as you realise this is nothing more than a small hiccup, all should be well. Let others do some of the work for you.

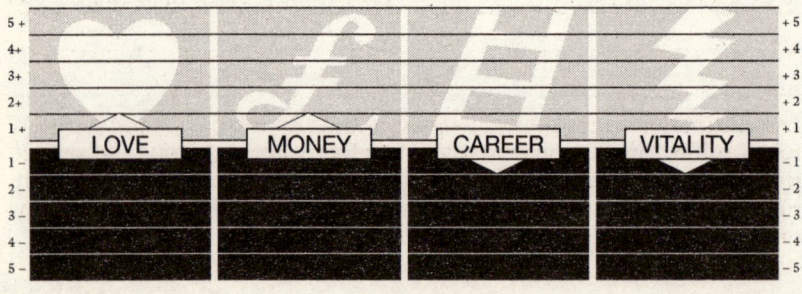

20 MONDAY   *Moon Age Day 28   Moon Sign Aquarius*

am ....

pm...

Stand back a little. If there are any frustrations about today, they are likely to come about as a result of the activities of others. Unfortunately, you will have to take these in your stride because there is very little you can do about them. A mixture of loyalty and Cancer sensitivity are most likely to prevent you from firing back.

21 TUESDAY   *Moon Age Day 29   Moon Sign Aquarius*

am ....

pm...

It looks as though this is a lucky time. Money-making endeavours are well starred and continue to be so for the next few days. Although you won't want to take too many chances, you do have the equivalent of an astrological guardian angel looking over you. When it comes to putting forward your unique point of view, tell it how it is.

22 WEDNESDAY   *Moon Age Day 0   Moon Sign Pisces*

am ....

pm...

The need for new input is strong just now and there isn't much doubt that your natural curiosity is extremely well honed. You should avidly devour even scraps of information that come your way in order to build up a better picture of the future. Allied to these trends is your ever-strengthening intuition.

23 THURSDAY   *Moon Age Day 1   Moon Sign Pisces*

am ....

pm...

Associations are what count now. You should enjoy the cut and thrust of relationships immensely today and tomorrow, and might gain a great deal simply from being around people you recognise as successful in their own right. You might detect a small but steadily growing desire to break out of some social or personal constraints.

24 FRIDAY
Moon Age Day 2   Moon Sign Pisces

am ....

pm...

Since professional progress appears to be rather limited, make the most of the fact that the influences favour a varied and interesting social life, so make sure you have somewhere to go this evening. Not everyone will turn out to be your friend, though it is hard to see what you have done to deserve it. Never mind – some people are just awkward!

25 SATURDAY
Moon Age Day 3   Moon Sign Aries

am ....

pm...

You need to be circumspect today. There are some jobs that are going to seem more trouble than they are worth. The reason for this is simple: you want to have fun and won't take at all kindly to being held back by anyone or anything. Decisive action is called for, even though you might be surprised by your own determination.

26 SUNDAY
Moon Age Day 4   Moon Sign Aries

am ....

pm...

Don't be too pushy at this time and avoid forcing your ideas on relatives and friends. By all means use a degree of persuasion, but in the end you must allow people to do things in their own way. The chances are that when you turn on the charm, you are likely to get your own way in any case. All it takes is that instinctive Cancer tactfulness.

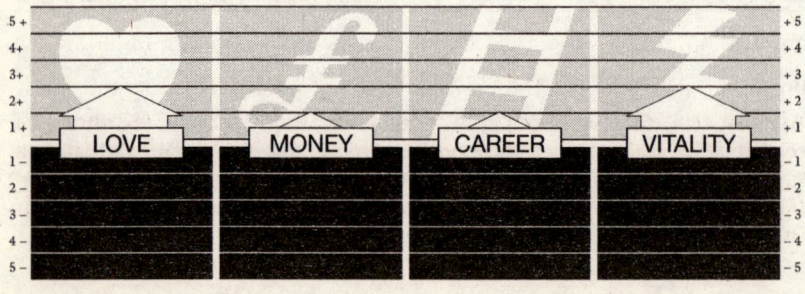

27 MONDAY
Moon Age Day 5   Moon Sign Taurus

am ....

pm...

You will enjoy excellent communication skills today and you would do well to use a lengthy discussion to help you to sort out problems that have been around for a while. Romance is a possibility for many Cancer subjects at this time, even if you may not be expecting it, so be alert to possibilities from an unexpected direction.

28 TUESDAY
Moon Age Day 6   Moon Sign Taurus

am ....

pm...

A little confusion could be on the way. Make sure you are not deceiving yourself when it comes to personal and even intimate decisions at present. It is possible that you need another point of view and there are people around who can deliver that for you. A little embarrassment is nothing if you feel very much better in the end.

29 WEDNESDAY
Moon Age Day 7   Moon Sign Taurus

am ....

pm...

This is a day when you won't take kindly to being told what to do. You need to be fairly tolerant, however, and not to blame the messenger when new instructions come along. Remember that others are only following the orders they have been given. It isn't like the Crab to be resentful, so make sure you avoid the temptation.

1 THURSDAY
Moon Age Day 8   Moon Sign Gemini

am ....

pm...

Love and romance occupy your mind, as your partner or sweetheart proves to be a good deal more responsive than might have been the case for a couple of days. You might decide to beat the last of the winter weather by putting your feet up in front of a roaring fire, though this strategy will only work for so long.

2 FRIDAY

Moon Age Day 9   Moon Sign Gemini

am ....

pm...

Family members may appear to think you are made of money, especially the younger ones. This means that you will have to tell them how things really are, which could elicit a little resentment and even some grumpy reactions before the day is out. Treat the whole thing with humour.

3 SATURDAY

Moon Age Day 10   Moon Sign Cancer

am ....

pm...

The Moon moves into your zodiac sign, bringing with it a greater determination and masses of popularity. Conversations of any sort can bring you more of what you want, so strike up discussions with everyone you meet. Today is a useful day and now is the time to take those hunches and to back them all the way.

4 SUNDAY

Moon Age Day 11   Moon Sign Cancer

am ....

pm...

You tend to be on the top of the world on what could be one of the best days of March, when other people will be finding you approachable and attractive. There could be some minor complications, probably in terms of romance, so it is important to approach whatever you wish to do with confidence.

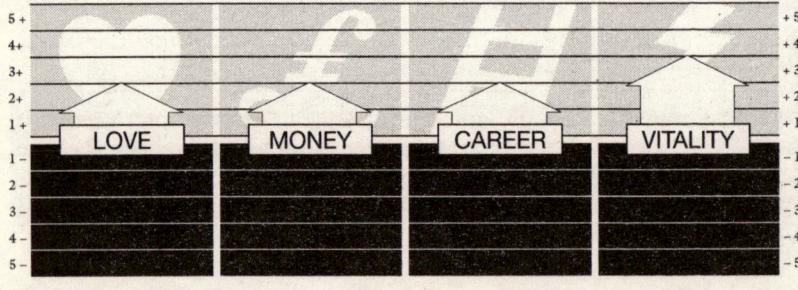

March

2012

YOUR MONTH AT A GLANCE

(+) = Opportunities are around   (—) = Be on the defensive   ● = Life is pretty ordinary

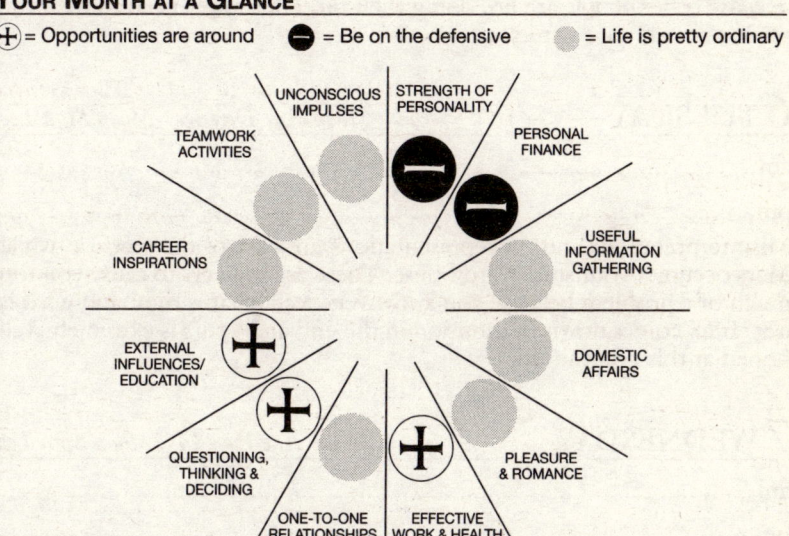

UNCONSCIOUS IMPULSES

STRENGTH OF PERSONALITY

TEAMWORK ACTIVITIES

PERSONAL FINANCE

CAREER INSPIRATIONS

USEFUL INFORMATION GATHERING

EXTERNAL INFLUENCES/ EDUCATION

DOMESTIC AFFAIRS

QUESTIONING, THINKING & DECIDING

ONE-TO-ONE RELATIONSHIPS

EFFECTIVE WORK & HEALTH

PLEASURE & ROMANCE

MARCH HIGHS AND LOWS

Here I show you how the rhythms of the Moon will affect you this month. Like the tide, your energies and abilities will rise and fall with its pattern. When it is above the centre line, go for it, when it is below, you should be resting. **HIGH 3RD–4TH**

HIGH 30TH–31ST

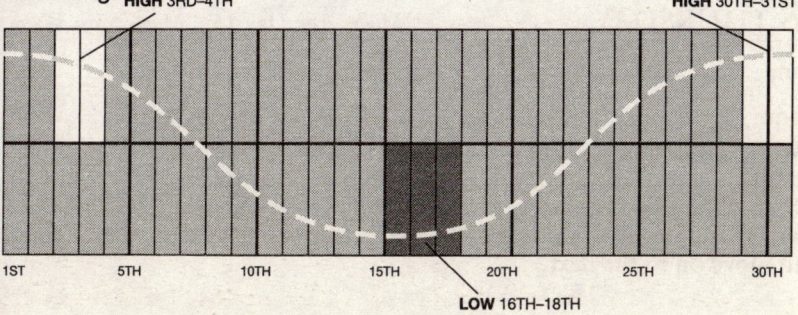

1ST   5TH   10TH   15TH   20TH   25TH   30TH

LOW 16TH–18TH

5 MONDAY
Moon Age Day 12   Moon Sign Leo

am ....

pm ....

This can be a great time to recognise opportunities that should be coming your way. Not everything is likely to turn out exactly as you would wish and there could be occasions when it is difficult for you to get ahead because other people are not doing their bit. You simply need to treat the situation with your natural patience.

6 TUESDAY
Moon Age Day 13   Moon Sign Leo

am ....

pm ....

Misinterpretations and misrepresentations are part of the scenario while Mars occupies your solar third house. These are unlikely to cause you too much of a problem because you know very well what is right and what is not. It all comes down to intuition in the end and yours is extremely well honed at this point in time.

7 WEDNESDAY
Moon Age Day 14   Moon Sign Leo

am ....

pm ....

You may be drawn towards new ideas at this time and you will certainly be showing a truly ingenious side to your nature. Away from the practical, you are in a very romantic frame of mind and should be doing all you can to make your partner feel happy and secure. If you don't have a partner, now is the time to look.

8 THURSDAY
Moon Age Day 15   Moon Sign Virgo

am ....

pm ....

Widen your horizons and make sure you get as much from life as possible, even though there are some slight irritations that threaten to hold you back. When it comes to getting jobs done, it would be best to proceed slowly and steadily, finishing each stage before you decide the time is right to move on to the next.

9 FRIDAY

Moon Age Day 16   Moon Sign Virgo

am...

pm..

There are high points in social proceedings that you won't want to miss today, together with good promise for a sociable few days and a great deal of optimism on your part. Because you are likely to be feeling good, you can show your most positive face to the world and your mood is infectious – if you smile, they will smile back.

10 SATURDAY

Moon Age Day 17   Moon Sign Libra

am...

pm..

Many good things should be happening around you now, even if some of them are not actually happening to you. That doesn't really matter because the Crab is one of the most generous-hearted signs of the zodiac. As long as those you care about are prospering, to a great extent you are making gains too – and that's what counts.

11 SUNDAY

Moon Age Day 18   Moon Sign Libra

am...

pm..

The positive side of the present position of Mars in your solar chart is that you are mentally astute and will be able to jump to conclusions long before certain other people even stop to think. Use this to your distinct advantage when it comes to getting ahead. It should also help you in any sporting endeavour.

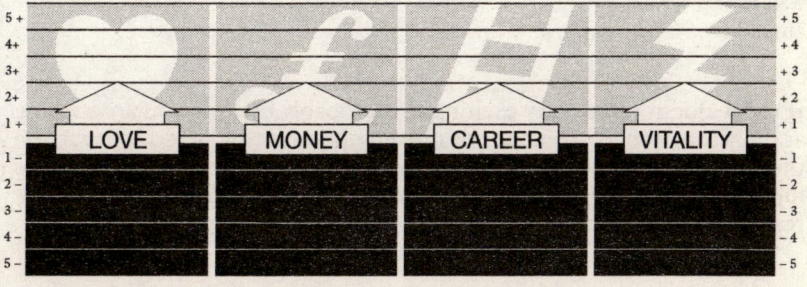

12 MONDAY ☿ *Moon Age Day 19 Moon Sign Scorpio*

am ....

pm ....

Long journeys, communications and other mental as well as social endeavours could all be important over the next few days. Establish new directions and get on with tasks that have been waiting a while because you are filled with energy and just raring to go. There is very little at the moment that will get in your way.

13 TUESDAY ☿ *Moon Age Day 20 Moon Sign Scorpio*

am ....

pm ....

Ensure that the way you work is both sensible and well considered. There is just a slight danger at present that you could be doing all manner of things that are out of sequence or not even necessary. People you don't see very often could be returning to your life at any time now and they could bring surprises with them.

14 WEDNESDAY ☿ *Moon Age Day 21 Moon Sign Sagittarius*

am ....

pm ....

Your eager mind will learn things very quickly under present trends and you are likely to be coming up with some fairly sensational ideas. The problem could be that you don't always have as much confidence as you need and so you should enlist the support and even the practical help of people who can assist you with your schemes.

15 THURSDAY ☿ *Moon Age Day 22 Moon Sign Sagittarius*

am ....

pm ....

If today doesn't look very exciting it is probably because you are looking at the wrong things. You need to remain optimistic and to concentrate on those matters that will lift your spirits. It would be best to get the tedious jobs out of the way first, leaving you more time later for pursuits that really stimulate your mind.

16 FRIDAY ☿ *Moon Age Day 23 Moon Sign Capricorn*

am ....

pm ....

You could experience a number of disappointments right now, possibly as a result of the lunar low. The daily structure of your life is being taken for granted by other people and you need to remind them, in your usual diplomatic way, that they are not doing what is required of them. Work offers few gains but some entertainment.

17 SATURDAY ☿ *Moon Age Day 24 Moon Sign Capricorn*

am ....

pm ....

It's true that there are likely to be situations today that will try your patience but you are quite capable of rising above difficulties and you can win through to your objectives despite the position of the Moon. The amount of effort you have to put in will be greater but the triumph will be that much more welcome too.

18 SUNDAY ☿ *Moon Age Day 25 Moon Sign Capricorn*

am ....

pm ....

Although the lunar low can still drain your energy at the start of today, it won't be long until you are back on form and able to look at the world in a positive frame of mind. Once again it is important not to get ahead of yourself and to concentrate your efforts on one job at a time. You work much more effectively if you build progressively.

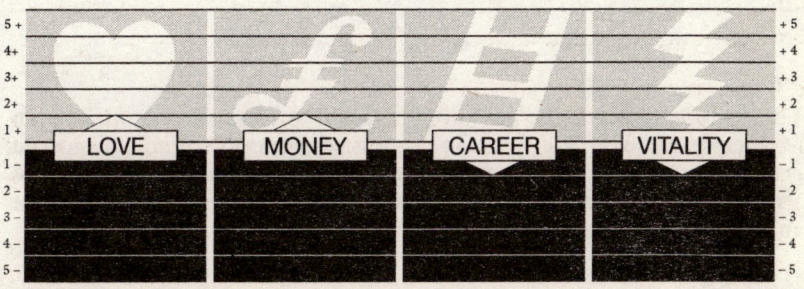

19 MONDAY ☿ *Moon Age Day 26   Moon Sign Aquarius*

am ....

pm...

As a Cancerian, charm is second nature to you, especially now, which makes this a very good time to ask for things you want. Your generally good-natured view of life is obvious to everyone and it would be difficult for those around you to refuse you any reasonable request. Look for a definite boost to your love life.

20 TUESDAY ☿ *Moon Age Day 27   Moon Sign Aquarius*

am ....

pm...

Domestic circumstances come good to such an extent that you probably won't want to be anywhere but at home. Don't be too quick to take offence if you are criticised in some way because there is a strong chance that most people are truly on your side now. In contrast, expect compliments from both expected and unexpected directions.

21 WEDNESDAY ☿ *Moon Age Day 28   Moon Sign Pisces*

am ....

pm...

With little real excitement in view this is the sort of day during which most matters will proceed pretty much as you might expect. Don't be too quick to judge others, either by their actions or through what they are saying. Jumping to conclusions could lead you into hot water, an even more likely scenario if you indulge in gossip.

22 THURSDAY ☿ *Moon Age Day 0   Moon Sign Pisces*

am ....

pm...

Thanks to fiery Mars, the pursuit of personal freedom is what makes you happiest today. You won't feel in the least comfortable if you are forced down paths that are not of your own choosing. Give and take in romantic attachments is another key to success at present, so be willing to look at an alternative point of view.

23 FRIDAY ☿ *Moon Age Day 1   Moon Sign Aries*

am...

pm...

In all probability you can look forward to warm responses from a host of people around you, not least those individuals you care for deeply. Young Cancerians, or those who have been actively looking for love, should not be disappointed at present. Bear in mind that you will almost certainly have to work hard in new or old relationships.

24 SATURDAY ☿ *Moon Age Day 2   Moon Sign Aries*

am...

pm...

In every real sense you are footloose and fancy-free today and in just the right frame of mind to get what you want. You don't achieve this objective by being difficult or pushy. On the contrary, you are sweetness itself and inclined to do as many good favours as there are hours in the day. That's what makes you so special.

25 SUNDAY ☿ *Moon Age Day 3   Moon Sign Taurus*

am...

pm...

In terms of the way you usually approach relationships of the heart, you could be feeling in a slightly contentious frame of mind today. In many respects you are probably more dominant and sure of yourself than has been the case for a while. Try to stay away from arguments that have nothing to do with you.

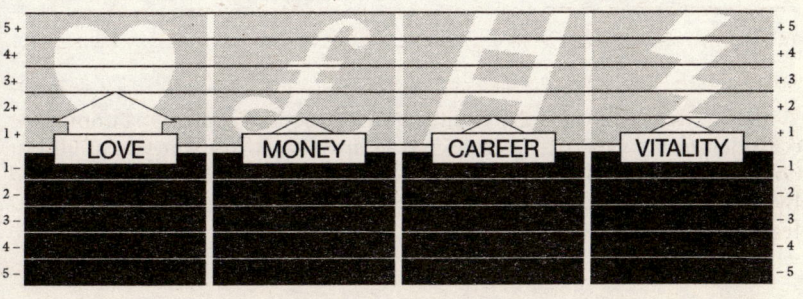

26 MONDAY ☿ *Moon Age Day 4   Moon Sign Taurus*

am ....

pm...

You can prosper by using your personal magnetism, which is quite strong now. A disruptive phase in work matters doesn't really matter too much because you should be dedicating most of today to having fun in one way or another. Plan holidays now, or if you are especially lucky, take a break from what might be a gloomy prospect outside.

27 TUESDAY ☿ *Moon Age Day 5   Moon Sign Taurus*

am ....

pm...

Positive thinking is around and you can happily depend on receiving help and support from others today if you only ask for it. Instead of struggling with matters you are not able to resolve, turn to someone who has more experience than you do. Even at a casual level, a conversation will carry instructions you simply have to follow.

28 WEDNESDAY ☿ *Moon Age Day 6   Moon Sign Gemini*

am ....

pm...

Thanks to Venus, this is a time of potential romantic promise. There is everything to gain from social involvement, most likely with people you fancy, or if you are already spoken for, types who fill you with a sense of wonder. All kinds of different people pay a visit to your life around now, and bring happiness with them.

29 THURSDAY ☿ *Moon Age Day 7   Moon Sign Gemini*

am ....

pm...

With the Moon in your solar twelfth house, freedom is the most important consideration today. Being restricted in any way won't suit you at all but could make you feel a type of personal claustrophobia if you are restrained by any circumstance. However, remember that you need to be patient, at least until tomorrow.

30 FRIDAY ☿ *Moon Age Day 8   Moon Sign Cancer*

am ....

pm ....

You have been hovering on the brink of significant progress for a few days now. The lunar high offers the extra incentive to take matters into your own hands and produce what you want from life. Even if that means being somewhat more selfish than usual, you could never completely forget about the needs of others.

31 SATURDAY ☿ *Moon Age Day 9   Moon Sign Cancer*

am ....

pm ....

All Crabs should be the life and soul of the party over the next couple of days and there is no reason why you should be any different so book events in your social diary. At work, certain situations could be trying, especially if you are expected to take on additional responsibilities or organise something that puts you in the spotlight.

1 SUNDAY ☿ *Moon Age Day 10   Moon Sign Cancer*

am ....

pm ....

The first day of April arrives and you will be nobody's fool this year. Although you could feel emotionally pressured into taking a particular course of action, you need to do what suits you best. In the end, this is the correct course of action because you can't achieve anything while you are living a lie. The lunar high is still present today.

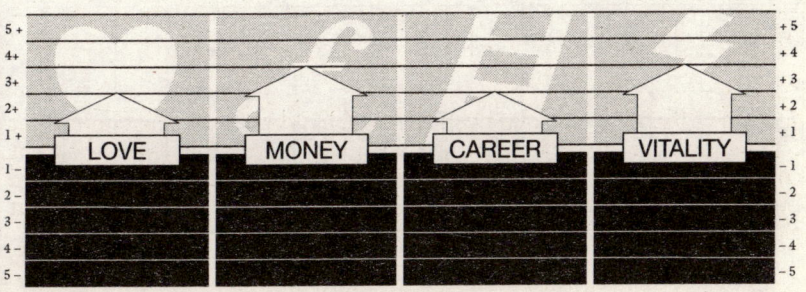

April

2012

YOUR MONTH AT A GLANCE

(+) = Opportunities are around   (—) = Be on the defensive   ⬤ = Life is pretty ordinary

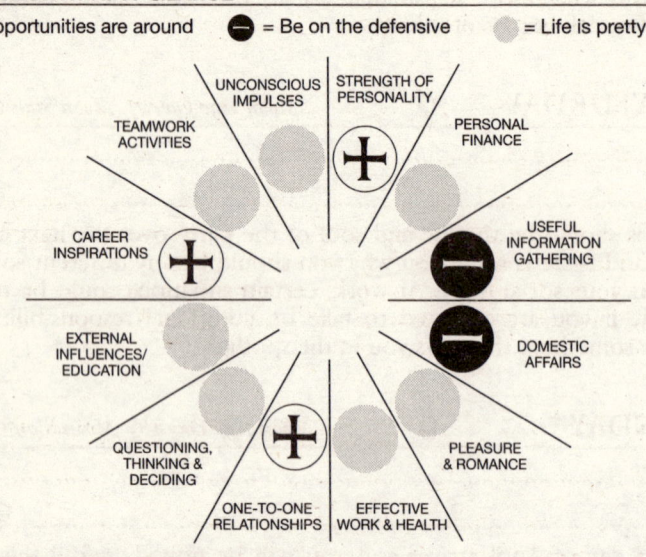

UNCONSCIOUS IMPULSES

STRENGTH OF PERSONALITY (+)

TEAMWORK ACTIVITIES

PERSONAL FINANCE

CAREER INSPIRATIONS (+)

USEFUL INFORMATION GATHERING (—)

EXTERNAL INFLUENCES/ EDUCATION

DOMESTIC AFFAIRS (—)

QUESTIONING, THINKING & DECIDING (+)

PLEASURE & ROMANCE

ONE-TO-ONE RELATIONSHIPS

EFFECTIVE WORK & HEALTH

APRIL HIGHS AND LOWS

Here I show you how the rhythms of the Moon will affect you this month. Like the tide, your energies and abilities will rise and fall with its pattern. When it is above the centre line, go for it, when it is below, you should be resting. HIGH 1ST

HIGH 27TH–28TH

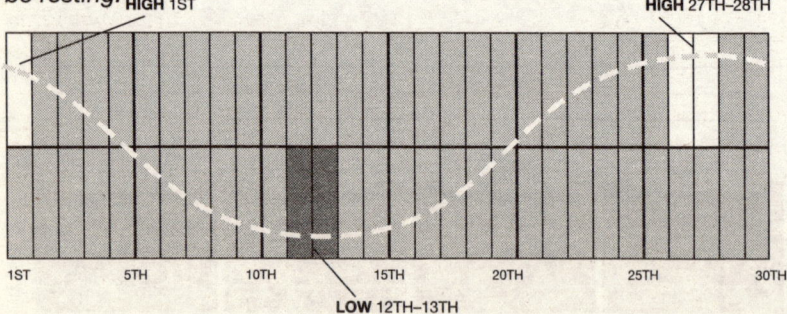

| 1ST | 5TH | 10TH | 15TH | 20TH | 25TH | 30TH |

LOW 12TH–13TH

2 MONDAY ☿ *Moon Age Day 11   Moon Sign Leo*

am ....

pm..

Today should feel generally secure. This is a period during which intimate and private matters should be a source of emotional fulfilment, always an important factor in the life of a Cancerian. There could be reasons to celebrate as a result of things happening within the family and you should be the first one to put out the flags.

3 TUESDAY ☿ *Moon Age Day 12   Moon Sign Leo*

am ....

pm..

Despite the fact that you may feel a number of obligations bearing down on you, today is good for all mental pursuits. Your mind is crystal clear and you can get through or around a number of potential obstacles. On the way, you are stretching yourself, which has to be a good thing under present trends.

4 WEDNESDAY ☿ *Moon Age Day 13   Moon Sign Virgo*

am ....

pm..

Domestic attachments and relationships are extremely important to you today, as they always are. Venus is in your solar eleventh house, constantly turning your mind back in the direction of your home and the people who live there. This would be a good time for entertaining, especially dinner parties or intimate social gatherings.

5 THURSDAY *Moon Age Day 14   Moon Sign Virgo*

am ....

pm..

Domestic issues still stand as being potentially more rewarding than outside interests. Present planetary trends cause you to cling tenaciously to home and family. You may also find that nostalgia rules today and you could enjoy thinking about the past and the good things it has brought you. Old friends are now the ones that count.

6 FRIDAY
Moon Age Day 15   Moon Sign Libra

am ....

pm...

This is a time to get down to business so today would be a good day to look very carefully at the practical side of life. You clearly have your thinking head on at the moment and will be able to resolve problems that are stumping others. Romance shows itself around this time, although it will pass you by if you are not observant.

7 SATURDAY
Moon Age Day 16   Moon Sign Libra

am ....

pm...

Romantic attachments remain positively highlighted now. Interesting encounters are also on the cards so be attentive to anything odd, unusual or curious. Be prepared to change direction at a moment's notice if your intuition tells you this would be the best thing to do. Get out and about over the next couple of days.

8 SUNDAY
Moon Age Day 17   Moon Sign Scorpio

am ....

pm...

Things that are both useful and practical turn out to be your main concern at the end of the weekend. Don't be frightened to say what you think, especially when you are in the company of people who have the ability to change things. By the evening, you could be in the market for some real fun so seek out those of a like mind.

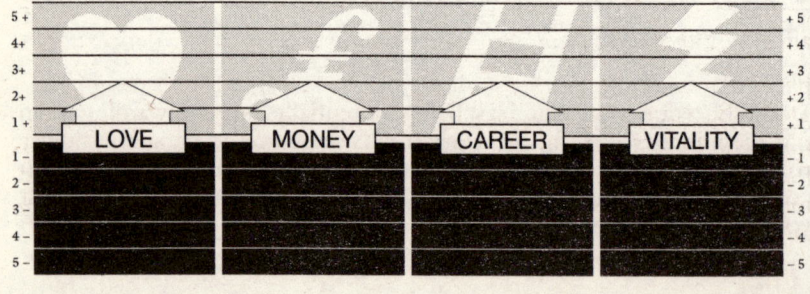

9 MONDAY

Moon Age Day 18   Moon Sign Scorpio

am...

pm...

Don't believe everything you hear today because there are some people around who have a vested interest in fooling you. Venus is now in your solar twelfth house and although this is not a difficult planetary position in a general sense, it can incline you to be slightly more gullible than would normally be the case.

10 TUESDAY

Moon Age Day 19   Moon Sign Sagittarius

am...

pm...

There could be issues around at work that you thought you had already dealt with, though in reality they will have to be looked at again. Be as diligent as possible today in pursuit of your aims and objectives and don't stop concentrating until you know things are finished properly. Look forward to a family time in the evening.

11 WEDNESDAY

Moon Age Day 20   Moon Sign Sagittarius

am...

pm...

Your mental judgement is good today and the progress you make should be slightly better than over the last couple of days. Mercury is on your side, which favours communication, especially when you are telling someone how much you care for them. Focus on not losing sight of the bigger picture by concentrating on the details.

12 THURSDAY

Moon Age Day 21   Moon Sign Capricorn

am...

pm...

A few irritations are inevitable when the lunar low comes along but in the main you should manage this period better than is sometimes the case. As long as you don't expect too much from today, you will be happy with the moderate progress you make because your view of life tends to be realistic at the moment.

13 FRIDAY
Moon Age Day 22   Moon Sign Capricorn

am ....

pm..

It would be best not to attempt anything too strenuous for the moment. Just keep yourself tuned into those tasks you know you can achieve without pushing yourself unduly. Offers that come in from outside could seem inviting but if they involve any sort of expenditure it might be best to leave them until tomorrow.

14 SATURDAY
Moon Age Day 23   Moon Sign Aquarius

am ....

pm..

The act of getting to the root of almost any issue is worth the effort, especially at a time when you are less than willing to settle for second best. Today can offer a great deal in terms of personal fulfilment and you should be open to the idea of discovering interesting new subjects and finding out about the lives of others.

15 SUNDAY
Moon Age Day 24   Moon Sign Aquarius

am ....

pm..

If you are not careful, you could be deceived by other people under present trends, mainly thanks to Venus in your solar twelfth house. In some respects you may be slightly unrealistic in your expectations of others and you could be disappointed if they let you down. However, you remain open-minded, cheerful and competent.

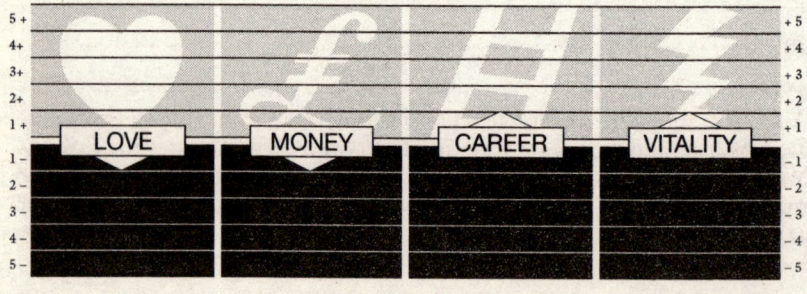

16 MONDAY   *Moon Age Day 25   Moon Sign Aquarius*

am..

pm..

Make long-term plans now while the planets favour looking ahead. Both travel and broadening your mind are on the cards and you are about to embark on a series of exciting departures in almost every sense of the word. Apply yourself in your everyday life as you now tend to be imaginative and inspirational.

17 TUESDAY   *Moon Age Day 26   Moon Sign Pisces*

am..

pm..

You ought to be fairly assertive at the moment and you will be inclined to tell people what you really think, which certainly isn't always the case for the Crab. In some ways you could find yourself at odds with the general consensus but you need to stick to your guns and will probably be proved right in the end.

18 WEDNESDAY   *Moon Age Day 27   Moon Sign Pisces*

am..

pm..

You have a lot of energy right now so you should throw yourself into professional challenges. For those who are out of work, make sure you keep looking as there is a good opportunity for something to come your way. You might end up following a path you never expected but the results could be extremely good.

19 THURSDAY   *Moon Age Day 28   Moon Sign Aries*

am..

pm..

You have an uncharacteristic desire to be prominent, which is so unusual it could take those around you completely by surprise. You are always willing to work extremely hard and to do whatever is necessary to achieve your objectives and break the bounds of what once seemed possible. You could be the only one who is surprised.

20 FRIDAY

Moon Age Day 29   Moon Sign Aries

am ....

pm ....

The Moon is in your solar tenth house and this allows you to confront and to deal with issues that have seemed difficult in the recent past. You tend to stick well to things right now and you won't be diverted from whatever path you have chosen just because someone else thinks it is not a good idea. You might even show a stubborn side.

21 SATURDAY

Moon Age Day 0   Moon Sign Aries

am ....

pm ....

A new lease of life is on the way for Cancerians who feel they have not achieved their best so far this year. Whether in a social or a professional dimension, you seem to be much more committed and able to do whatever it takes to get noticed. Your upfront attitude is refreshing and should attract positive attention from other people.

22 SUNDAY

Moon Age Day 1   Moon Sign Taurus

am ....

pm ....

Keep your options open when it comes to making important decisions and keep up the pressure to show an unsuspecting world what you are capable of achieving. It's fine to be single-minded but only up to a point. If you realise that you are travelling in the wrong direction it is sensible to turn around and to look for a new way forward.

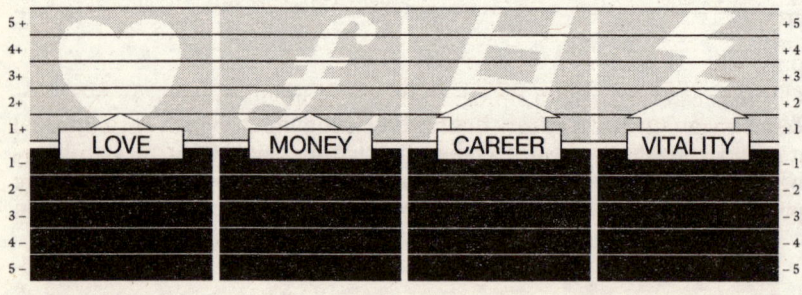

23 MONDAY
Moon Age Day 2   Moon Sign Taurus

am ....

pm ....

It looks as though there could be strong emotions to deal with today, though few of them are likely to be exhibited by you. It seems as though everyone has a unique and somewhat awkward point of view, which itself could lead to some disagreements. As usual, you will be expected to be the one who negotiates the compromise.

24 TUESDAY
Moon Age Day 3   Moon Sign Gemini

am ....

pm ....

In a way untypical of Cancer, you could find yourself being critical of others today, although only where important decisions are concerned. The fact is that you are right not to go blindly into any situation as it demonstrates that you are being discriminatory. This is especially important in terms of financial commitments.

25 WEDNESDAY
Moon Age Day 4   Moon Sign Gemini

am ....

pm ....

People are turning to you for help and advice of a sort they feel only you can offer. Today may be good from a financial point of view, particularly as a result of actions you took some time ago which are only now bearing fruit. What matters for today is that you give full rein to your versatility.

26 THURSDAY
Moon Age Day 5   Moon Sign Gemini

am ....

pm ....

Getting your own way in almost all situations could turn out to be rather easier than you had expected. Simply turn on the charm, put forward a good, reasoned case and wait for the result. A degree of frugality may be necessary in the short term, if only to prove to others that you can practically live on fresh air.

27 FRIDAY
Moon Age Day 6   Moon Sign Cancer

am ....

pm ....

You have all the support you require today with which to push your ideas forward. Any tendency to retreat into your own little world now disappears and you find yourself happy to be in the social flow and taking your place in the world. You should be able to count on good luck brought to you by the lunar high.

28 SATURDAY
Moon Age Day 7   Moon Sign Cancer

am ....

pm ....

The lunar high remains around and where there have previously been problems, you should notice situations changing rapidly for the better. Good luck attends most of your efforts and you won't have to push yourself too hard to get where you want to go. Relationships of a personal nature are beginning to look especially good.

29 SUNDAY
Moon Age Day 8   Moon Sign Leo

am ....

pm ....

After two busy days, you may decide that the limelight is not at all where you want to be. Whether this turns out to be the case really depends on circumstances. If you find yourself pushed forward, particularly with regard to matters you understand well, you will simply have to take the stage – and you will perform well.

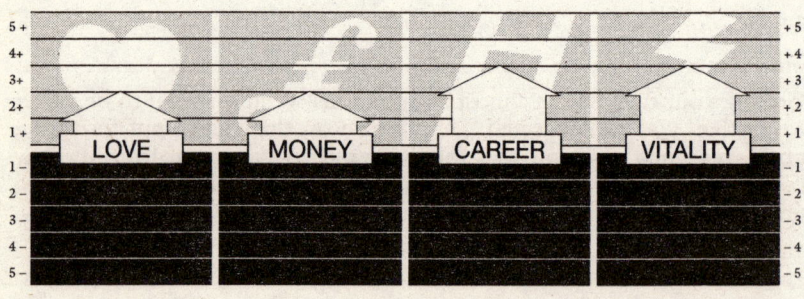

30 MONDAY

Moon Age Day 9   Moon Sign Leo

am...

pm...

Be careful because relationships can throw up the odd challenge and make it difficult for you to have the clear path ahead that you seem to need. Small problems come along and it's up to you to deal with them one at a time. What you should not be doing right now is taking on more than you can reasonably be expected to cope with.

1 TUESDAY

Moon Age Day 10   Moon Sign Virgo

am...

pm...

This is a week when you should go all out towards achieving your major ambitions because the planetary influences favour success in getting what you want from life. What you might find harder is to make certain people like you, if it seems that this is not the case. Simply be patient and you will bring them round.

2 WEDNESDAY

Moon Age Day 11   Moon Sign Virgo

am...

pm...

In all probability, creative pursuits will suit you down to the ground today. Maybe you are thinking about changes you want to make to your home, or just possibly contributing to a major refurbishment somewhere else, perhaps at work. You are very co-ordinated at the moment and this is reflected in your good taste.

3 THURSDAY

Moon Age Day 12   Moon Sign Virgo

am...

pm...

Many Cancerians are now feeling footloose and fancy-free, although hopefully that will not apply to the personal life of those in steady relationships! Nevertheless, the usual places and faces won't hold too much appeal for you, so try to take a trip, or find a way to demonstrate the original qualities of your nature.

4 FRIDAY
Moon Age Day 13   Moon Sign Libra

am..

pm..

For all sorts of reasons this is likely to be a day of preparation and you should be looking carefully at all eventualities before you decide to move in any specific direction. Keep an eye open if you are going to the shops. There are bargains around at present and you are in just the right frame of mind to snap some of them up.

5 SATURDAY
Moon Age Day 14   Moon Sign Libra

am..

pm..

A continued emphasis on practical issues sees you taking the next couple of days by the scruff of the neck and getting all sorts of jobs done. That won't suit everyone but it's impossible to do so at the moment. Money matters ought to be taking a turn for the better, with promising financial prospects showing up all the time.

6 SUNDAY
Moon Age Day 15   Moon Sign Scorpio

am..

pm..

You may opt for a quieter day than you had originally intended, though there is no likelihood that boredom will be part of the scenario. On the contrary, you are quite keen to look at new possibilities but it would be best to keep them in the planning stage, rather than racing out to do anything at least for a day or two.

	LOVE	MONEY	CAREER	VITALITY

May

2012

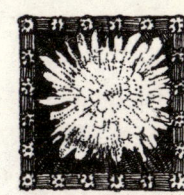

YOUR MONTH AT A GLANCE

➕ = Opportunities are around ➖ = Be on the defensive ⬤ = Life is pretty ordinary

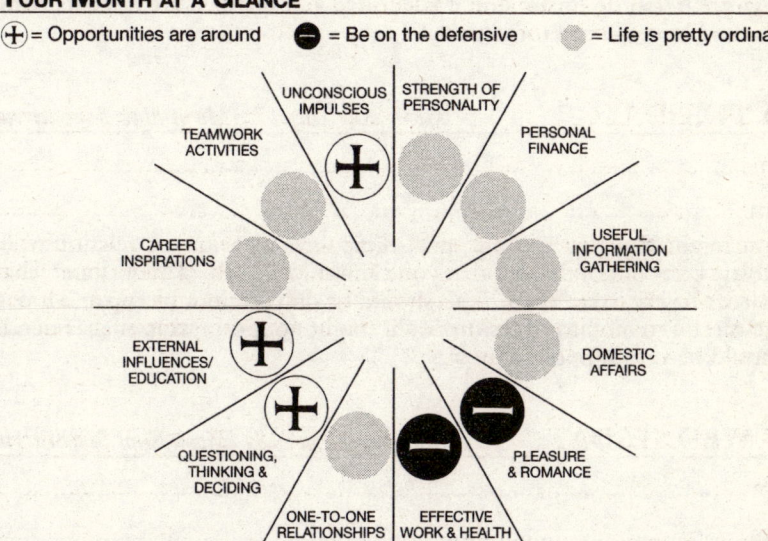

UNCONSCIOUS IMPULSES

STRENGTH OF PERSONALITY

TEAMWORK ACTIVITIES

PERSONAL FINANCE

CAREER INSPIRATIONS

USEFUL INFORMATION GATHERING

EXTERNAL INFLUENCES/ EDUCATION

DOMESTIC AFFAIRS

QUESTIONING, THINKING & DECIDING

PLEASURE & ROMANCE

ONE-TO-ONE RELATIONSHIPS

EFFECTIVE WORK & HEALTH

MAY HIGHS AND LOWS

Here I show you how the rhythms of the Moon will affect you this month. Like the tide, your energies and abilities will rise and fall with its pattern. When it is above the centre line, go for it, when it is below, you should be resting.

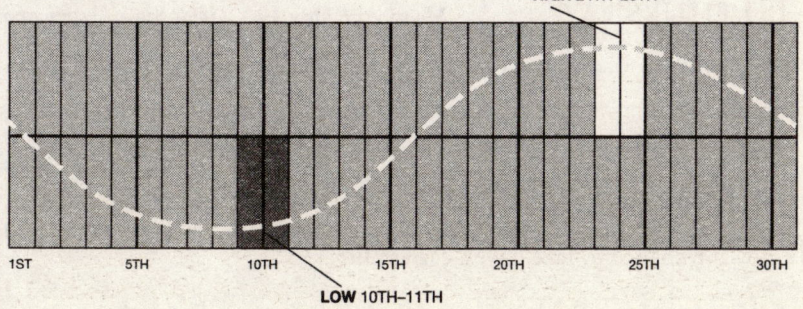

HIGH 24TH–25TH

1ST 5TH 10TH 15TH 20TH 25TH 30TH

LOW 10TH–11TH

7 MONDAY
Moon Age Day 16   Moon Sign Scorpio

am ....

pm..

Health matters could be uppermost in your mind at the start of this week and if so you can thank that twelfth house Venus. It's important to watch your diet at the moment and you may be thinking about starting a new regime. If you do, make sure it is sensible and that you are not expecting too much of yourself too quickly.

8 TUESDAY
Moon Age Day 17   Moon Sign Sagittarius

am ....

pm..

You might experience some small difficulties in romantic relationships, mostly born out of the fact that you cannot make others understand what you are trying to tell them. This should be only a minor hiccup and if you are careful to monitor the situation it might not be an issue at all. Friends should be very supportive now.

9 WEDNESDAY
Moon Age Day 18   Moon Sign Sagittarius

am ....

pm..

By tomorrow things are likely to slow down somewhat so it might be sensible today to make sure you have everything finished and that you initiate new plans. In a social sense you should be right on form and keen to mix freely, even with people you don't know very well. Any customary shyness disappears under present trends.

10 THURSDAY
Moon Age Day 19   Moon Sign Capricorn

am ....

pm..

Don't be surprised if you are short of energy for the next couple of days – take a back seat and be happy to let others do most of the work while you do some watching and thinking. To try to push any grandiose scheme through at the moment would be virtually impossible, so you may as well enjoy the chance to take a well-earned break.

11 FRIDAY
Moon Age Day 20   Moon Sign Capricorn

am ....

pm...

Necessary adjustments, adaptations and demands on your time today can crowd in on you if you allow them to do so. Instead of reacting by trying to do everything at once, you need to stay relaxed and to let life flow around you. Most of what causes a panic whilst the lunar low is around turns out to be nothing but a paper tiger.

12 SATURDAY
Moon Age Day 21   Moon Sign Aquarius

am ....

pm...

There may still be a little tension around today but bear in mind that even if this is the case, it won't last long. There are subtle changes taking place in your solar chart that will allow you to adapt quickly to changing circumstances. When it comes to love, you are certainly likely to be turning a few heads, one or two of which might surprise you.

13 SUNDAY
Moon Age Day 22   Moon Sign Aquarius

am ....

pm...

Look out for the odd difference of opinion, which is likely to be caused by the present position of Mars in your solar third house. The good side of this planetary position is that it gives you the ability to win arguments – not that you will be likely to start any. That's not your way, but it's good to know you have the answers you need.

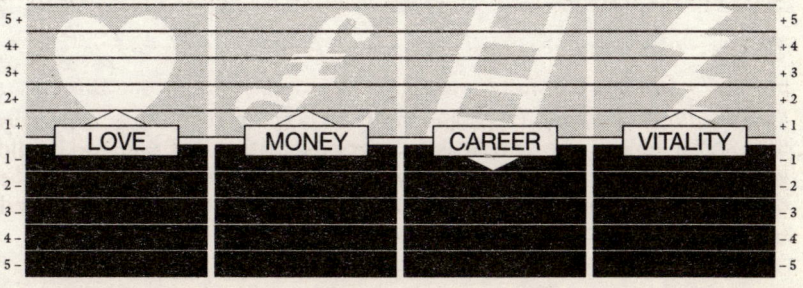

14 MONDAY
Moon Age Day 23   Moon Sign Pisces

am ....

pm..

There is a good chance that you could form new friendships around this time, especially with people who might help to expand your horizons and who can fulfil your present need for debate and intellectual discussion. You have your really clever head on right now and some of what you have to say is tinged with a kind of genius.

15 TUESDAY
Moon Age Day 24   Moon Sign Pisces

am ....

pm..

Though new commitments now are not based on the most secure foundation, you can muddle along somehow and you have what it takes to bluff your way through if necessary. You will be at your best when forced to think on your feet and won't be as nervous as usual about having to speak in public or argue your point.

16 WEDNESDAY
Moon Age Day 25   Moon Sign Aries

am ....

pm..

Be careful that you are not deluding yourself at the moment, especially when it comes to relationships. You may be too willing to sacrifice the truth for the sake of a loved one and this is a course of action that can only lead to difficulties later. Even if it means a slight upset to the ones you love, you need to be truthful.

17 THURSDAY
Moon Age Day 26   Moon Sign Aries

am ....

pm..

You should now have more opportunity to do your own thing, especially in a social sense. The Moon is in a good position for you today and you will positively insist on having your own way. People don't generally expect the Crab to be pushy – in fact it is so unusual that they are unlikely to argue any point about which you feel strongly.

18 FRIDAY
Moon Age Day 27   Moon Sign Aries

am ....

pm...

It is little things that are likely to get on your nerves today, so much so
that you will need to be careful not to be touchier than normal. The
reason is the position of Mars in your solar chart, though the fiery planet
does at least bestow on you the ability to tell it like it is. Once again,
people will be shocked and may well cave in immediately.

19 SATURDAY
Moon Age Day 28   Moon Sign Taurus

am ....

pm...

Today would be a great time for participating in group activities and for
getting together with like-minded people whenever you can. When it
comes to a project you have been undertaking, you might now have to
make some significant modifications at the last minute. This tends to be
something you don't really like to do.

20 SUNDAY
Moon Age Day 0   Moon Sign Taurus

am ....

pm...

What you can't do for yourself at this juncture, it is quite likely that friends
will be more than happy to do for you. Asking for help and support is not
a sin and since you are always so ready to put yourself out for everyone
else, there is no reason why people should refuse when you need a hand.
In reality, most of them will be delighted.

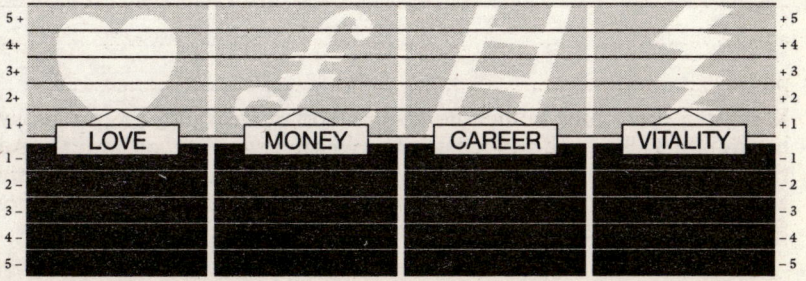

21 MONDAY
Moon Age Day 1   Moon Sign Gemini

am ....

pm..

As is often the case for the Crab, there ought to be great co-operation at home, even from younger people, one or two of whom could easily have been going through a rebellious streak in the recent past. If you can't get what you want at work by simply asking, some more drastic, though probably witty, solution may be necessary.

22 TUESDAY
Moon Age Day 2   Moon Sign Gemini

am ....

pm..

It might not be very easy to try to make personal relationships work out exactly as you would wish today. It is other people who seem to be awkward at present and who simply will not adopt what you see as being a rational point of view. It may be best to stick with friends for the moment and to leave deeper attachments alone.

23 WEDNESDAY
Moon Age Day 3   Moon Sign Gemini

am ....

pm..

The Sun is moving on all the time and today you will get better results from your efforts. You do need to push hard towards your objectives and to retain a slight sense of urgency regarding something you know to be of significance. As the days pass, so you start to feel invigorated and more inclined to work yourself harder.

24 THURSDAY
Moon Age Day 4   Moon Sign Cancer

am ....

pm..

When the lunar high comes along on a spring weekend, the prognosis has to be excellent. All you must remember today is that you won't make full use of your potential sitting around and doing nothing. Get out and about as much as possible and make the most of all new opportunities that come your way.

25 FRIDAY
Moon Age Day 5   Moon Sign Cancer

am ....

pm ....

The lunar high is still around and what an excellent time this would be for putting the finishing touch to fresh and innovative ideas. Remain determined and overthrow obstacles that might normally get in your way. Confidence levels remain generally high and it is clear that you have a number of things on your agenda at present.

26 SATURDAY
Moon Age Day 6   Moon Sign Leo

am ....

pm ....

In all probability you are very anxious to broaden your horizons in just about any way that proves possible. Romance is beckoning for many people born under the sign of the Crab and the arrival of the weekend offers new chances to make a good impression. Don't be surprised if you feel a little off colour early in the day.

27 SUNDAY
Moon Age Day 7   Moon Sign Leo

am ....

pm ....

This is a day for positive social relations, and for coming to terms with the changing ideas and attitudes of your family. Focus on personal contact, as the influences are so strong, and let practical matters take a back seat. Be sure to tell your partner, or those closest to you, how much they mean to you and to prove it in some way.

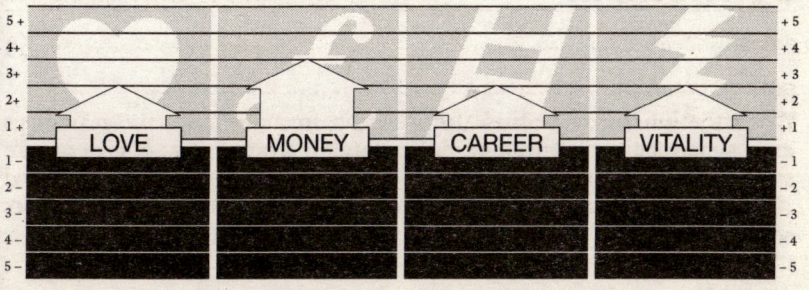

28 MONDAY
Moon Age Day 8   Moon Sign Leo

am ....

pm...

As a new week gets started, a few reliable long-term plans are now beginning to mature. You can afford to look at the broader picture of life and won't be so held back by immediate concerns as may have been the case recently. Be willing to listen to a rational point of view today, even if it comes from an unexpected direction.

29 TUESDAY
Moon Age Day 9   Moon Sign Virgo

am ....

pm...

Thanks to the present position of Mars in your solar chart, there is a degree of restlessness to deal with today. How you go about addressing this fact is up to you but you won't help the situation by settling yourself down to a whole host of boring routines. Off with the old and on with the new seems to be the best adage now.

30 WEDNESDAY
Moon Age Day 10   Moon Sign Virgo

am ....

pm...

The Crab now experiences a strong thirst for new experience. It will feel as if this is a response to the advancing year, though in reality the position of Mars is playing a part in the situation. Family members do things that make you both happy and proud, whilst you make every effort to repay what you consider to be an old debt.

31 THURSDAY
Moon Age Day 11   Moon Sign Libra

am ....

pm...

Pay attention today because information from colleagues, or perhaps even superiors, could prove to be very useful around now. It is definitely time to keep your eyes and ears open and to react quickly to changing circumstances. Some people are difficult to predict as the week moves on, so use your strong intuition to keep abreast of things.

1 FRIDAY
Moon Age Day 12   Moon Sign Libra

am...

pm...

It is just possible there will be intimate issues to deal with today. If you take these too seriously there is a chance they could get you down, which is not to be recommended. Maybe you ought to avoid dealing with anything too deep at the moment, opting instead for a more 'general' view of life, with all its various hues.

2 SATURDAY
Moon Age Day 13   Moon Sign Scorpio

am...

pm...

As is often the case, you are ready to make concessions to others, even to people who have clearly messed you about in the recent past. That doesn't mean you are knuckling under in any way, something you will be very loath to do with the present position of Mars. What you are actually up to is establishing compromise.

3 SUNDAY
Moon Age Day 14   Moon Sign Scorpio

am...

pm...

A loved one is likely to need some sensitive handling today but luckily you should have sufficient natural calm to deal with almost any situation. It's time for a good old-fashioned chat, either with a family member, your partner or a friend. If you have recently decided on any health regime, take things steadily for a while.

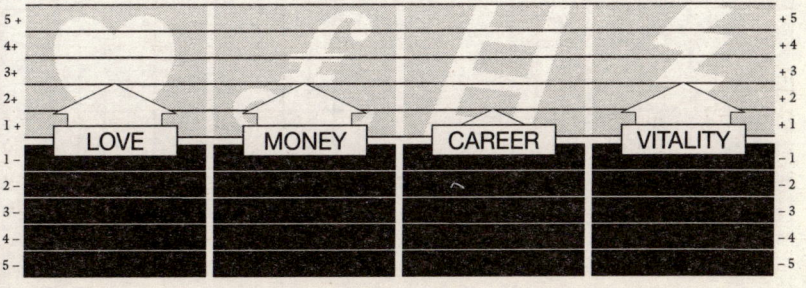

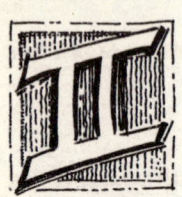

June

2012

Your Month at a Glance

$\bigoplus$ = Opportunities are around $\bigominus$ = Be on the defensive   ⬤ = Life is pretty ordinary

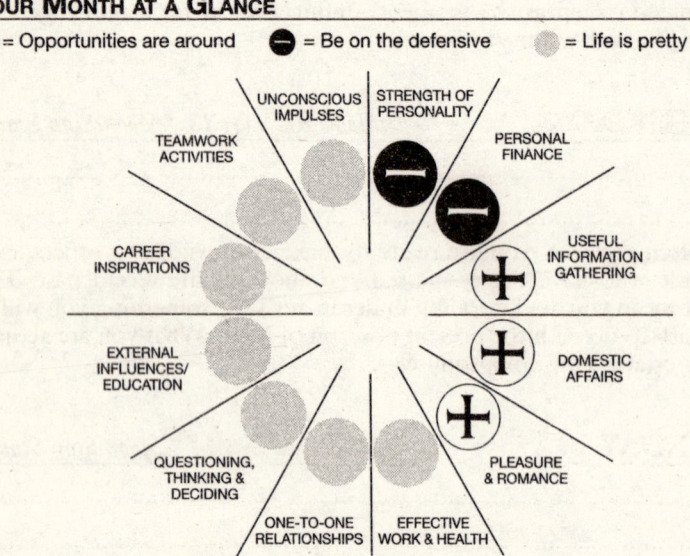

UNCONSCIOUS IMPULSES

STRENGTH OF PERSONALITY

TEAMWORK ACTIVITIES

PERSONAL FINANCE

CAREER INSPIRATIONS

USEFUL INFORMATION GATHERING

EXTERNAL INFLUENCES/ EDUCATION

DOMESTIC AFFAIRS

QUESTIONING, THINKING & DECIDING

PLEASURE & ROMANCE

ONE-TO-ONE RELATIONSHIPS

EFFECTIVE WORK & HEALTH

June Highs and Lows

Here I show you how the rhythms of the Moon will affect you this month. Like the tide, your energies and abilities will rise and fall with its pattern. When it is above the centre line, go for it, when it is below, you should be resting.

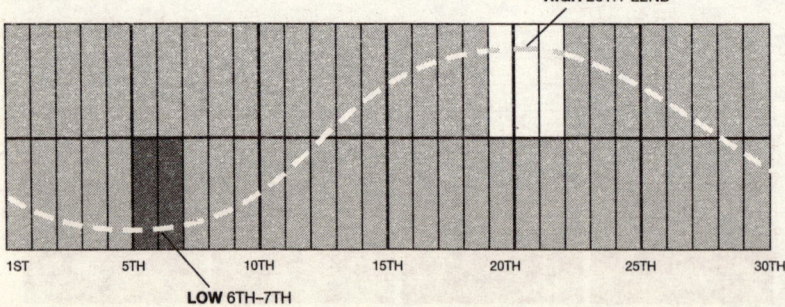

HIGH 20TH–22ND

1ST   5TH   10TH   15TH   20TH   25TH   30TH

LOW 6TH–7TH

4 MONDAY
Moon Age Day 15   Moon Sign Sagittarius

am ....

pm...

You could be required to make some fairly vital changes to your life at any time now and you need to be ready for these. Keep your eye on the ball, especially at work, and don't be found lacking when it comes to taking action. Someone you don't see very often could be making a surprise visit to your life very soon.

5 TUESDAY
Moon Age Day 16   Moon Sign Sagittarius

am ....

pm...

Avoid hasty speech for the moment and make sure that all your comments are well considered. There's a chance you could unintentionally upset someone and if this happens you would be the one who suffers in the long-run because you have such an active conscience. Travel plans are likely at almost any stage this week.

6 WEDNESDAY
Moon Age Day 17   Moon Sign Capricorn

am ....

pm...

There can be a few difficulties while the lunar low is around but in the main you are well prepared at this time and so you are unlikely to be taken by surprise by any sudden misfortune. On the contrary, you could be a great deal more optimistic and potentially successful than is usually the case at this stage of the month.

7 THURSDAY
Moon Age Day 18   Moon Sign Capricorn

am ....

pm...

Perseverance is crucial if you want to keep moving forward and to make the sort of impression on the world at large that is so important to you right now. It might not be too easy today because you may lack some of the support you generally take for granted. Keep an open mind about a friend who seems to be going off the rails.

8 FRIDAY

Moon Age Day 19   Moon Sign Aquarius

am ....

pm...

You could be slightly more impressionable and sensitive than usual today but as the hours pass you will be getting more into gear and moving further away from the lunar low. The Moon begins to work more positively on your behalf and you will feel more like stretching yourself. A good heart-to-heart at home could work wonders.

9 SATURDAY

Moon Age Day 20   Moon Sign Aquarius

am ....

pm...

A communication matter could prove tiresome in some way, leaving you deciding that there are times when it would be best to keep quiet. Some disputes are likely to rise to the surface but these can only have a bearing on you if you choose to take part in them. There are occasions today when you will be happy to keep your counsel.

10 SUNDAY

Moon Age Day 21   Moon Sign Pisces

am ....

pm...

The Sun is presently in your solar twelfth house, which is not the best position in terms of personal success and gain. Things improve markedly after around the 20th of this month and in the meantime you will simply have to keep plodding on. From a personal perspective this is a fairly fortunate time and you take shelter at home.

LOVE	MONEY	CAREER	VITALITY

11 MONDAY
Moon Age Day 22   Moon Sign Pisces

am ....

pm...

To a great extent your best course of action would be to fall back on your own reserves and not rely too heavily on other people. That is probably because you find them either difficult to deal with or slightly unreliable. Confidence is increasing but have patience as the pace of the change tends to be both slow and erratic.

12 TUESDAY
Moon Age Day 23   Moon Sign Pisces

am ....

pm...

The Moon helps you a little more at work now, although there seem to be conditions attached to everything you try to do, which can be slightly frustrating. Things should still be going well on the home front and you could have significant reason to feel proud of a family member at this time. Take time out for hobbies today.

13 WEDNESDAY
Moon Age Day 24   Moon Sign Aries

am ....

pm...

With that twelfth house Sun you are more inclined than usual to withdraw into your own inner world, which makes you less accessible to those close to you. If there are questions being asked of you it would be best not to defer the answers until a later date. You need to be quite truthful, though not at the complete expense of diplomacy.

14 THURSDAY
Moon Age Day 25   Moon Sign Aries

am ....

pm...

Mercury is moving ahead of the Sun and has already contacted your solar first house. This is better in terms of communication and also increases your self-esteem at a time when it really matters. You are also now willing to listen to what other people have to say and to react positively to suggestions that are being made, especially at work.

15 FRIDAY
Moon Age Day 26   Moon Sign Taurus

am ....

pm..

Venus remains in your solar twelfth house, which is a slightly other-worldly position for the planet of love. As a result you could be slightly dreamier in your view of romance and maybe not entirely realistic in your expectations of others. Keep plodding away at the practical aspects of life because these do support you.

16 SATURDAY
Moon Age Day 27   Moon Sign Taurus

am ....

pm..

Because you are developing really strong views about quite a few matters, there are times today when it would definitely be best not to push your ideas forward too much. People might take offence that you don't intend to offer and that would lead to disputes or arguments you can easily do without at this stage of the month.

17 SUNDAY
Moon Age Day 28   Moon Sign Taurus

am ....

pm..

Make a point of searching your feelings before you offer a response or make an important decision. It's true that there are always practical matters to consider but at the end of the day you won't do anything well if you find it awkward or even repulsive. Now is a time for compromise and this comes thick and fast.

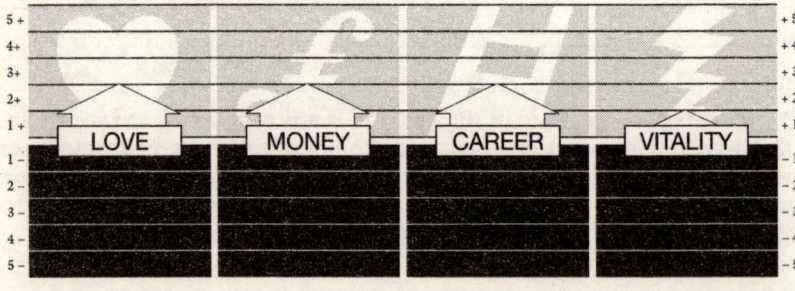

18 MONDAY
Moon Age Day 29   Moon Sign Gemini

am ....

pm ....

Heart-warming encounters with all manner of people are likely to enliven your life today. The sensitive side of Cancer is never very far from the surface and shows especially well in your dealings with your partner, or close family members of whom you are inordinately fond. Keep a weather eye on business transactions.

19 TUESDAY
Moon Age Day 0   Moon Sign Gemini

am ....

pm ....

There could be a few disagreements to overcome right now and it might be suggested that getting involved in arguments in the first place is something of a waste of time. You would be better advised to go to almost any lengths to keep the peace. This will probably mean biting your tongue, but that is something that comes easily to you.

20 WEDNESDAY
Moon Age Day 1   Moon Sign Cancer

am ....

pm ....

This is clearly time to push ahead rapidly with your dreams and schemes. There ought to be a great deal of support from the world at large, but specifically from relatives and friends. The presence of the lunar high is inclined to allow you greater latitude in the way you put your message across to others so speak your mind.

21 THURSDAY
Moon Age Day 2   Moon Sign Cancer

am ....

pm ....

It is hard to imagine a better set of circumstances for you. The lunar high is on your side and at the same time the Sun is moving into your solar first house. Keep up your efforts to get ahead, both at work and socially, and enjoy the cut and thrust of a life that should be feeling less restricted and a good deal more exciting.

22 FRIDAY

Moon Age Day 3   Moon Sign Cancer

am ....

pm..

The Moon stays in Cancer and today should bring you to a definite mental peak and one that will prove to be especially important in the days and weeks ahead. Some plans come to fruition at this time, leaving you with plenty of time to plan new moves. Any sort of balancing act is especially easy to deal with under prevailing trends.

23 SATURDAY

Moon Age Day 4   Moon Sign Leo

am ....

pm..

Today's very positive planetary focus bodes well for a change of scenery. An early holiday might suit you down to the ground and would offer the sort of diversion you are looking for at this time. Be alert to the fact that even casual conversations can lead you towards the sort of knowledge that is going to be useful before very long.

24 SUNDAY

Moon Age Day 5   Moon Sign Leo

am ....

pm..

You should opt for a complete change of scenery if this is at all possible. Staying in the same place is likely to bore you. Meanwhile the more competitive and sporting side of your nature is on display. Most important of all, you simply want to enjoy yourself and you have the ability to help others to do the same.

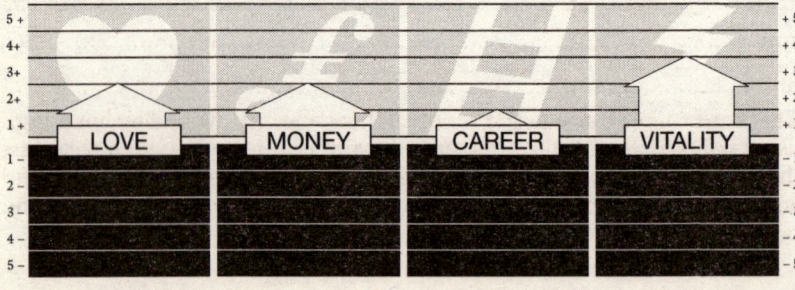

25 MONDAY   *Moon Age Day 6   Moon Sign Virgo*

am ....

pm...

Attending to a variety of tasks will not be at all hard at the beginning of this week. You are able to look at life with a very practised eye and will be hardly likely to come up against problems that you fail to address successfully. At work you not only do your own work, but some that rightfully belongs to others too.

26 TUESDAY   *Moon Age Day 7   Moon Sign Virgo*

am ....

pm...

It is important to pay attention today and if you can stay on the right side of people with power, you won't do yourself any harm at all. This doesn't have to involve being a 'creep', but merely means showing how polite you can be. Casual conversations potentially lead to new ideas and a partnership of some sort could be in the offing.

27 WEDNESDAY   *Moon Age Day 8   Moon Sign Libra*

am ....

pm...

The middle of this week brings further possibilities in terms of travel and ideal opportunities to get some fresh air. If you are a sporting Crab, you may be donning your shorts and competing in some way, though no matter what your proclivities, you get a better chance to enjoy yourself when away from routines.

28 THURSDAY   *Moon Age Day 9   Moon Sign Libra*

am ....

pm...

The world looks good and you will find plenty of people on your wavelength today. Of course you can't expect that this will be universally the case. It is important to realise that some people are never going to adopt your point of view. Stop trying to make converts and concentrate on relationships that are already going well.

29 FRIDAY
Moon Age Day 10   Moon Sign Scorpio

am ....

pm..

It is true that you have the ability to get on well in a practical sense, but that won't necessarily please everyone. The way to deal with such eventualities is to be diplomatic. No amount of arguing is going to get you what you want now and you need to be flexible in your attitude, which is second nature for the Crab.

30 SATURDAY
Moon Age Day 11   Moon Sign Scorpio

am ....

pm..

It may occur to you this weekend that in a financial sense you could now be somewhat in the dark. If other people are running the show, you will have to ask a few leading questions. On a more personal front, you could easily be about to come across someone who you find immensely attractive. The feeling is likely to be mutual.

1 SUNDAY
Moon Age Day 12   Moon Sign Sagittarius

am ....

pm..

With the Sun in your first house, you seem to be the life and soul of the party now and will be having a good time at any social event. All the time you grow in confidence and feel yourself achieving objectives that would have seemed impossible once upon a time. You can afford to gloat a little but there is still much to be done.

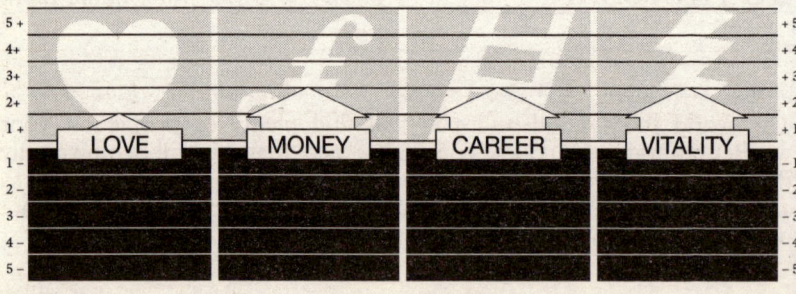

July

2012

$\bigoplus$ = Opportunities are around $\bigominus$ = Be on the defensive   ● = Life is pretty ordinary

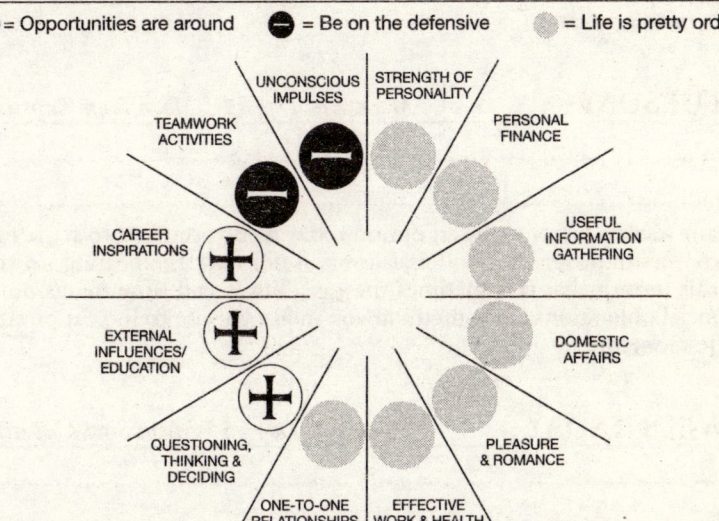

UNCONSCIOUS IMPULSES

STRENGTH OF PERSONALITY

TEAMWORK ACTIVITIES

PERSONAL FINANCE

CAREER INSPIRATIONS

USEFUL INFORMATION GATHERING

EXTERNAL INFLUENCES/ EDUCATION

DOMESTIC AFFAIRS

QUESTIONING, THINKING & DECIDING

PLEASURE & ROMANCE

ONE-TO-ONE RELATIONSHIPS

EFFECTIVE WORK & HEALTH

JULY HIGHS AND LOWS

Here I show you how the rhythms of the Moon will affect you this month. Like the tide, your energies and abilities will rise and fall with its pattern. When it is above the centre line, go for it, when it is below, you should be resting.

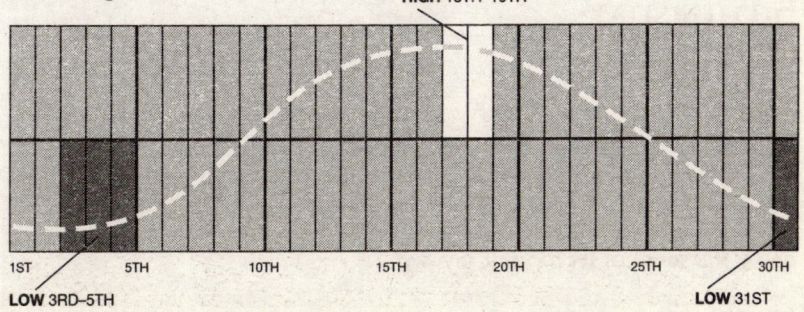

HIGH 18TH–19TH

1ST   5TH   10TH   15TH   20TH   25TH   30TH

LOW 3RD–5TH

LOW 31ST

2 MONDAY   *Moon Age Day 13   Moon Sign Sagittarius*

am..

pm..

Look after small matters on the work front and allow others to take care of themselves. You can't have everything that you want from life right now, but in many respects you can come very close. When making any sort of repair, make sure you do it thoroughly and then you won't have more problems later.

3 TUESDAY   *Moon Age Day 14   Moon Sign Capricorn*

am..

pm..

Instant success is not really an option today so be prepared to settle for a steady sort of progress. The lunar low will not have the bearing on your life this month that is sometimes the case, but it will slow things down. Financial obligations are something you might choose to look at carefully at the moment.

4 WEDNESDAY   *Moon Age Day 15   Moon Sign Capricorn*

am..

pm..

Things may not be progressing very well today and a go-slow policy may seem to be in operation but don't allow yourself to get depressed because this is just the influence of the lunar low. In a couple of days you'll be back to your own vibrant self. In the meantime, enjoy the slower pace and use the fact that it gives you more time to think.

5 THURSDAY   *Moon Age Day 16   Moon Sign Capricorn*

am..

pm..

A domestic or family matter could appear to be too confining today and you will be longing to get away, maybe into the country or, better still for you, to the coast. If you can find some time to take a trip, then do so. You might choose to take a close friend or your partner with you and really enjoy the sense of freedom it gives you.

6 FRIDAY   *Moon Age Day 17   Moon Sign Aquarius*

am ....

pm..

Cancer is really on form today and you should demonstrate your keen perception and shrewd judgement, two factors that are bound to assist you on your march through life. Look out for exciting possibilities and don't turn down the chance to do something quite daring. Personally, you know what you want and can now get it.

7 SATURDAY   *Moon Age Day 18   Moon Sign Aquarius*

am ....

pm..

If you work today you could now be making decisions that will have far-reaching consequences. However, you can't spend all day working and there's a good chance that you will be making the most of leisure hours in order to please yourself. Look out for a bargain if you embark on a shopping trip.

8 SUNDAY   *Moon Age Day 19   Moon Sign Pisces*

am ....

pm..

It is possible that difference facets of your life come together today. For example, you can't differentiate between your home life and work. Looking and planning ahead, you can achieve a better sense of balance, whilst at the same time using at least part of Sunday to come to terms with close relatives and even a friend or two.

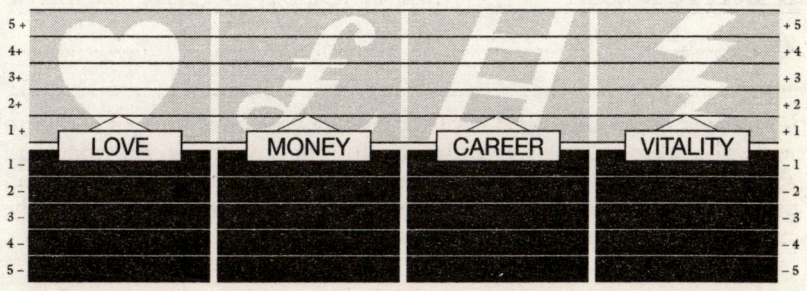

9 MONDAY
Moon Age Day 20   Moon Sign Pisces

am ....

pm ....

In your daily life there are further pleasant encounters to be expected and lots of fun for the taking. Nothing should be viewed too seriously this week because there are plenty of jokers around – in fact you are chief amongst them. Get out and about if you can because some sort of journey would suit you down to the ground.

10 TUESDAY
Moon Age Day 21   Moon Sign Aries

am ....

pm ....

Now you are in a good position to bring important matters to a head. You won't take kindly to people interfering in your life, particularly on a personal level. Although your zodiac sign doesn't go looking for confrontation, a few people could be about to discover that you are no pushover.

11 WEDNESDAY
Moon Age Day 22   Moon Sign Aries

am ....

pm ....

Your persuasive powers are strong and if there is something you particularly want to do, don't hold back. Most people will gladly follow your lead at this time, even though you are clearly making up your mind as you go along. Use the fact that the sheer magnetism of your personality is on display for everyone to see.

12 THURSDAY
Moon Age Day 23   Moon Sign Taurus

am ....

pm ....

This could be another good day for chancing your arm. When it comes to cash, you seem to have the Midas touch right now and so the odd small flutter might be in order. During these early days of July you should find you are able to make significant progress and be more than able to take on several different projects at the same time.

13 FRIDAY

Moon Age Day 24   Moon Sign Taurus

am...

pm...

The Sun is still with you and so Friday the thirteenth is not likely to be at all unlucky for you. On the contrary, you should find that this is a distinctly go-ahead period, and a time when you can look out for all sorts of new possibilities hovering on the fringes of your life. Look for support from colleagues, who should be extremely helpful.

14 SATURDAY

Moon Age Day 25   Moon Sign Taurus

am...

pm...

It will be necessary to make some compromises today and you may not find that easy. However, if you stop to think first, it should be possible to get what you want and to please a number of other people on the way. Just remember, there is more than one way to get what you want and you can surely find the best way to achieve your ends.

15 SUNDAY   ☿

Moon Age Day 26   Moon Sign Gemini

am...

pm...

For a couple of days it could seem as though everyone is getting ahead faster than you are, and to a certain extent this is true, for today at least. However, this quieter spell does not last very long and you can manage to curb your enthusiasm for just a short time. Conversation in the evening could prove to be extremely interesting.

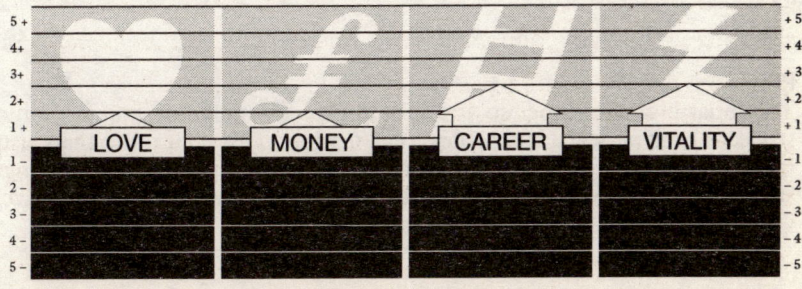

16 MONDAY ☿ *Moon Age Day 27   Moon Sign Gemini*

am..

pm...

Patience is still necessary because there are some irritations to deal with right now, although if you keep your frustrations to yourself – which you are likely to do – most people won't even realise you are feeling out of sorts. There are people who will guess all the same. These are likely to be family members, who know you very well.

17 TUESDAY ☿ *Moon Age Day 28   Moon Sign Gemini*

am..

pm...

Things improve and this is likely to be a highly entertaining and satisfying period on the work front, though it may have less going for it personally. Stick with those who give you the fairest hearing, even though these might be people you don't know very well. A distinctly sporting side to your nature is well favoured now.

18 WEDNESDAY ☿ *Moon Age Day 29   Moon Sign Cancer*

am..

pm...

Most of your everyday endeavours should be running fairly smoothly and your general level of good luck is certainly higher than it was earlier in the month. If you feel like a flutter, then go ahead. Backing the wrong horse is not especially likely today in any situation, though of course some caution is still necessary.

19 THURSDAY ☿ *Moon Age Day 0   Moon Sign Cancer*

am..

pm...

The lunar high continues so you should take advantage of your winning streak in both personal and professional matters. This is far more than just the monthly lunar high, because now you have the planet Mars pulling strongly for you. With energy to spare, lots of ideas available and a positive view of the world, it's onward and upward.

20 FRIDAY ☿ *Moon Age Day 1   Moon Sign Leo*

am ....

pm ....

Venus is now well placed for anyone looking for love. This is a good time to look for happy romantic encounters. It is possible that an admirer you never suspected you had is about to turn up. Reconsider your attitude to someone who has teased you recently – they might turn out to have fancied for you for some time.

21 SATURDAY ☿ *Moon Age Day 2   Moon Sign Leo*

am ....

pm ....

The weekend finds you eager to spread your wings and maybe to fulfil plans you laid down earlier in the week. Although it is clear that you want to be what other people expect, it is most important right now to please yourself too. Try to avoid giving the wrong impression when you are in company.

22 SUNDAY ☿ *Moon Age Day 3   Moon Sign Virgo*

am ....

pm ....

There are plenty of people about who will offer you innumerable compliments, but you must learn not to be unduly modest and to accept them graciously. Spend at least part of today concentrating on having a good time. All you have to do to make the most of today is to be confident and be yourself.

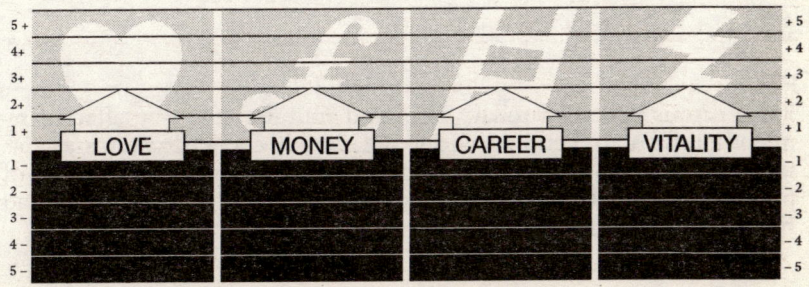

23 MONDAY ☿ *Moon Age Day 4   Moon Sign Virgo*

am ....

pm ....

There is strength in your chart. This is a time for revitalising elements of your personal life and for getting them going in a direction that suits you. Clear the decks for new action in a practical sense and don't be in the least surprised if you discover that you are doing most of the work today. It isn't forced upon you – you choose it.

24 TUESDAY ☿ *Moon Age Day 5   Moon Sign Libra*

am ....

pm ....

Beware all you Cancerians. This is hardly a time for taking yourself, or those around you, too seriously. Much that happens at this time has a very humorous edge to it, so be prepared to laugh at life, and at yourself if necessary. The brightest and best qualities of your zodiac sign are now on display – so use them to the full.

25 WEDNESDAY ☿ *Moon Age Day 6   Moon Sign Libra*

am ....

pm ....

If you are offered new responsibilities you should not turn them down out of hand. Having confidence in your own abilities is what today is all about and there are gains to be made if you ask the right questions. Career prospects are very good and you need to show what you are made of to superiors.

26 THURSDAY ☿ *Moon Age Day 7   Moon Sign Libra*

am ....

pm ....

Some care is necessary today. Work and routines could be affected by minor mishaps. It helps to check and double-check situations at this time and to avoid embarking on anything too adventurous. A sense of proportion in matters of love can be particularly useful and you will find that your friends are still especially helpful.

27 FRIDAY ☿ *Moon Age Day 8 Moon Sign Scorpio*

am..

pm..

A new phase begins that enhances all aspects of work and practical life. The Sun is now really shining for you, and does so for the next couple of weeks. In hard-and-fast terms this helps you to get things done and also provides just the mental stimulus you need to get on with new projects.

28 SATURDAY ☿ *Moon Age Day 9 Moon Sign Scorpio*

am..

pm..

Use your day wisely and don't spend all of it catching up with mundane chores, some of which can definitely wait. When dealing with loved ones, standard responses won't work too well at present and you need originality. The world of leisure and pleasure is anything but boring to you around now.

29 SUNDAY ☿ *Moon Age Day 10 Moon Sign Sagittarius*

am..

pm..

The opportunities to prove yourself come thick and fast. You are flexible, easy-going and good to know at present. Don't be in the least surprised if you find compliments coming from all sorts of directions. This is definitely not a stay-at-home sort of day. It's time to show the world what you are made of.

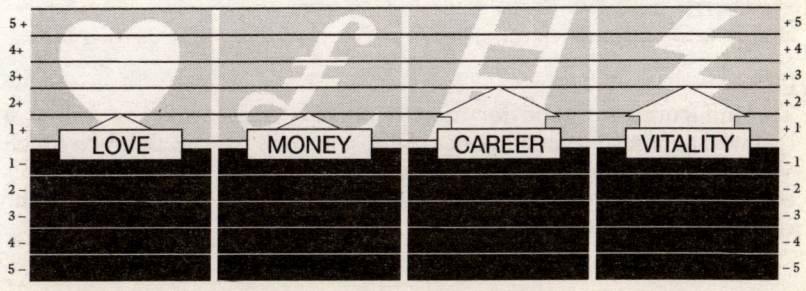

30 MONDAY ☿ *Moon Age Day 11* *Moon Sign Sagittarius*

am ....

pm...

Avoid making life difficult for others and especially your partner or those closest to you. For today at least you are not in the best frame of mind and it may be a good idea to spend a little time on your own. Creative potential remains quite good and this might be an ideal time to cheer up your home or to take on a new hobby.

31 TUESDAY ☿ *Moon Age Day 12* *Moon Sign Capricorn*

am ....

pm...

You may feel the everyday obligations of life tend to press in on you right now. It would be a good time to take some time out, if only to think through some of the potential open to you. With the lunar low about, it would be sensible to deal with a few little jobs before clearing the decks for another progressive period ahead.

1 WEDNESDAY ☿ *Moon Age Day 13* *Moon Sign Capricorn*

am ....

pm...

You may still have to pace yourself a good deal as far as work is concerned. However, by the time the afternoon arrives you should be feeling back to your old self again. Get in gear and do something. Try an exciting departure that you have shied away from in the past and marvel at your new courage.

2 THURSDAY ☿ *Moon Age Day 14* *Moon Sign Aquarius*

am ....

pm...

The influences are good for new friendships at this time, as well as a renewed approach to existing ties. Almost anyone has the ability to touch a part of you because you are presently so sensitive. Social discussions could now prove enlightening if you pay attention and you will relish the company of interesting types.

3 FRIDAY ☿ *Moon Age Day 15   Moon Sign Aquarius*

am...

pm...

There may not have been time recently to do everything you would have wished. Although today is busy too, there ought to be moments to do someone a good turn. The Crab is always available to offer help and advice and today is no exception. You ought to find that younger people especially are enjoying your company.

4 SATURDAY ☿ *Moon Age Day 16   Moon Sign Pisces*

am...

pm...

Solving certain problems has never been easier. You have a mind like Sherlock Holmes at present and should not dismiss your most intense feelings about anything. Analytical and yet at the same time sensitive to nuances, your ability to get inside the skin of those around you is especially highlighted today.

5 SUNDAY ☿ *Moon Age Day 17   Moon Sign Pisces*

am...

pm...

Practically speaking, you should be getting on with your plans today, and most likely involving others on the way. This ought to be a fairly relaxed sort of day and a time when you will be happy to do some of those chores that have been waiting in the wings for a while now. You are perfectly happy to plod along with life.

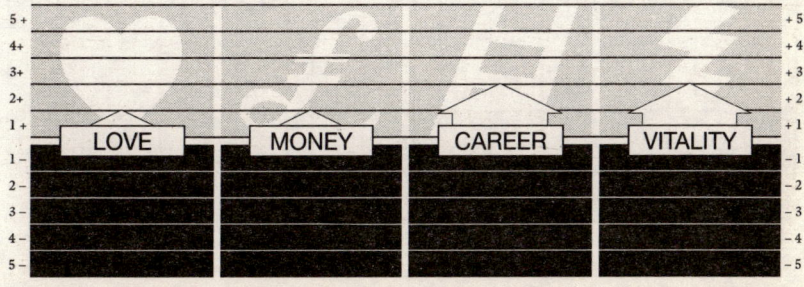

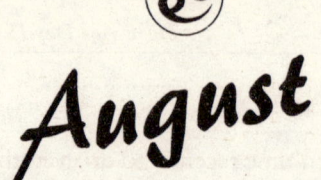

2012

Your Month at a Glance

⊕ = Opportunities are around   ⊖ = Be on the defensive   ● = Life is pretty ordinary

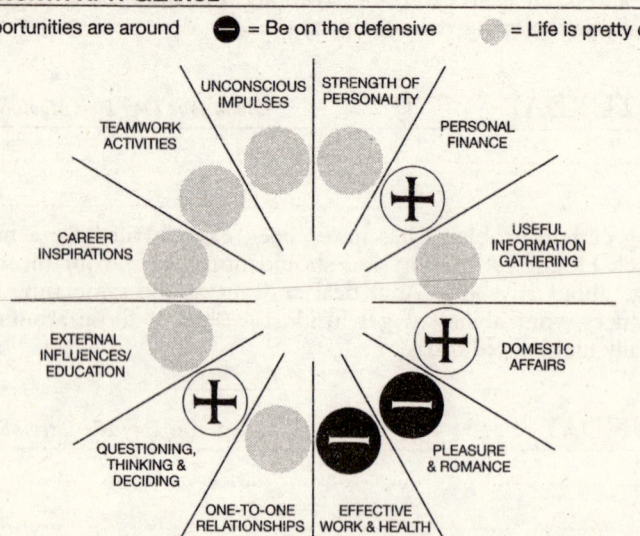

UNCONSCIOUS IMPULSES

STRENGTH OF PERSONALITY

TEAMWORK ACTIVITIES

PERSONAL FINANCE

CAREER INSPIRATIONS

USEFUL INFORMATION GATHERING

EXTERNAL INFLUENCES/ EDUCATION

DOMESTIC AFFAIRS

QUESTIONING, THINKING & DECIDING

PLEASURE & ROMANCE

ONE-TO-ONE RELATIONSHIPS

EFFECTIVE WORK & HEALTH

August Highs and Lows

Here I show you how the rhythms of the Moon will affect you this month. Like the tide, your energies and abilities will rise and fall with its pattern. When it is above the centre line, go for it, when it is below, you should be resting.

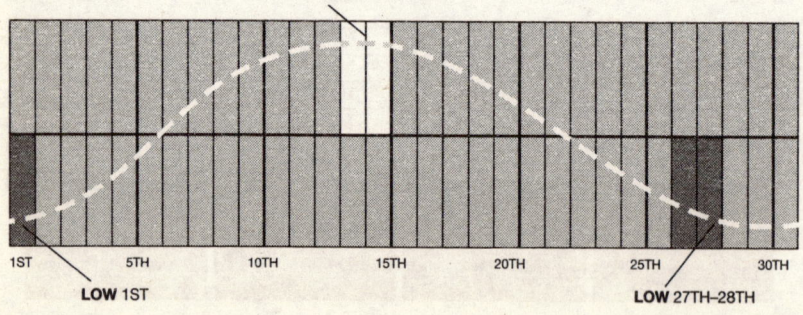

HIGH 14TH–15TH

1ST   5TH   10TH   15TH   20TH   25TH   30TH

LOW 1ST

LOW 27TH–28TH

6 MONDAY   ☿   *Moon Age Day 18   Moon Sign Aries*

am ....

pm ....

A good start to the week because your ego can be well and truly boosted today, as much as anything by the remarks others are making. Although there are ongoing jobs that have to be done, in some ways you are taking a refreshingly new look at life. As a result, rearrangements are much more likely at this time.

7 TUESDAY   ☿   *Moon Age Day 19   Moon Sign Aries*

am ....

pm ....

Be sure to be on the lookout for those who come new to your life at this time. This could either be at work or later in your social life. These people might be about to bring a message with them that you will be wise to take on board. In reality, advice on your life and circumstances is all around you at this time if you pay attention.

8 WEDNESDAY   ☿   *Moon Age Day 20   Moon Sign Aries*

am ....

pm ....

There's no doubt about it: keeping on the move is the best way to stay happy today. You should be cheerful, with a joking attitude and a breezy nature, even to situations that might normally get you down. Staying flexible is important and you should not allow yourself to be bogged down by domestic routines, most of which can wait.

9 THURSDAY   *Moon Age Day 21   Moon Sign Taurus*

am ....

pm ....

The Crab is really working well at this time. There are good things happening today and you can be part of them. It really depends on your state of mind from the very start of the day. It would be sensible to take a very optimistic view because what you project at the moment has a great bearing on the way events turn out.

10 FRIDAY
Moon Age Day 22   Moon Sign Taurus

am ....

pm..

Look around you because there are influences about that put you in touch with the wider social world now. Confirmation of something you suspected is coming in later in the day, though you have to concentrate to realise the fact. You remain busy, generally happy and quite keen to make some sort of splash.

11 SATURDAY
Moon Age Day 23   Moon Sign Gemini

am ....

pm..

This is another of those periods when you find it quite easy to deal with several jobs at the same time. Don't be too eager to take on board the problems of the world though. It's true that you almost always want to be of assistance, but at the end of the day you can't live the lives of others for them, so avoid too much interference.

12 SUNDAY
Moon Age Day 24   Moon Sign Gemini

am ....

pm..

Home is the best and most comfortable place for the Crab to be at present, so this could be a good day for not moving around too much. You are quite creative at the moment so will probably be working in your house or garden. A degree of personal contentment is present at this time, even if you are somewhat quiet.

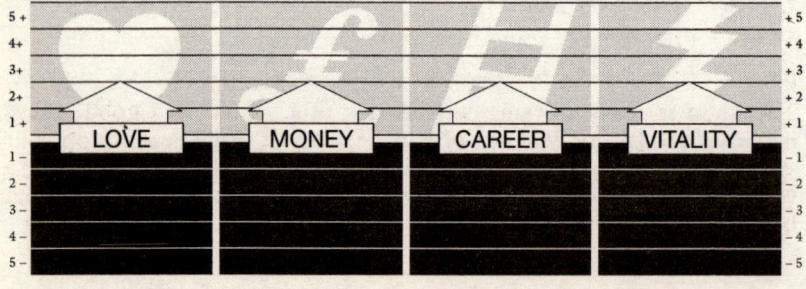

13 MONDAY
Moon Age Day 25   Moon Sign Gemini

am ....

pm...

This will probably not be the most dynamic few days you have encountered recently. The Moon is in your solar twelfth house and that makes you pensive and slightly withdrawn. Don't worry though because this interlude will certainly not last long. There are good things in store and some arrive before the end of the day.

14 TUESDAY
Moon Age Day 26   Moon Sign Cancer

am ....

pm...

One of the most productive and happy periods you have experienced for some time has arrived. If you don't feel good and get on well right now, you probably are not trying very hard. There is more than a little luck attending most of your actions and what matters most about today is being around people you really like.

15 WEDNESDAY
Moon Age Day 27   Moon Sign Cancer

am ....

pm...

Not only the people you know but individuals you have barely met before conspire to give you a good day. This is not a time for routines. The lunar high demands that you put in that extra bit of effort that can make all the difference. With good luck on your side, getting along well is easy and money matters should look good too.

16 THURSDAY
Moon Age Day 28   Moon Sign Leo

am ....

pm...

The emphasis remains on fun and games, allowing you to show a much less stressed face to the world at large. You'll find that self expression is very easy, which is one of the reasons you are now more relaxed. Not everyone you meet appears inclined to treat you fairly but you can use your intuition to sort out the wheat from the chaff.

17 FRIDAY
Moon Age Day 0   Moon Sign Leo

am ....

pm ....

The planets are still with you and help seems available to you today, no matter what you decide to do. There are times when you are responding to necessity rather than to choice, but you can make these enjoyable too. Routines could be a bore, which is why you should be doing your best to ring the changes as much as you can.

18 SATURDAY
Moon Age Day 1   Moon Sign Leo

am ....

pm ....

This may be one of the best potential periods for financial gain during August. You tend to act very much on impulse today but your sense of humour is fully in place and so if you make a mistake, you can laugh your way out of it. Concern for the underdog is particularly strong at the moment and you want to help all you can.

19 SUNDAY
Moon Age Day 2   Moon Sign Virgo

am ....

pm ....

With your powers of attraction now in the ascendant, make the most of the situation. If you are single, you should find attention coming from a number of different directions, though of course this could be the case even if you are not single. As far as you are concerned, responsibilities are for the birds right now.

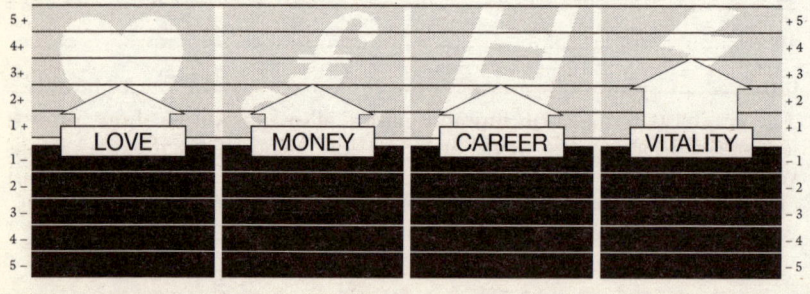

20 MONDAY
Moon Age Day 3   Moon Sign Virgo

am ....

pm..

Things are lining up well for you and now is as good a time as ever to take your life into your own hands. You clearly know what you want and have a very good idea about how you are going to get it. Even apparently unfortunate events can be turned to your advantage and will give you a racing start as August really gains pace.

21 TUESDAY
Moon Age Day 4   Moon Sign Libra

am ....

pm..

At this stage of the month, the focus is still predominantly on leisure and it is fair to say you may not be in the mood for too much work today. Do what is necessary but keep the best part of the day for simply enjoying yourself. It won't help to take either yourself or anyone else too seriously at present.

22 WEDNESDAY
Moon Age Day 5   Moon Sign Libra

am ....

pm..

It looks as though you will be open to new input right now and would be pleased to try things you have shied away from in the past. There are some genuine personalities about and you are not the least amongst them. With a great urge to find fresh fields and pastures new, this is the best time of all to think about a holiday.

23 THURSDAY
Moon Age Day 6   Moon Sign Scorpio

am ....

pm..

It might be best to avoid being too impulsive in financial matters and to save some money for later. You may have to get up early today in order to get everything necessary done and out of the way. This is important because later in the day you will want to do what takes your own fancy.

24 FRIDAY
Moon Age Day 7   Moon Sign Scorpio

am..

pm..

Today marks a time when you can get the best from others, and a period during which you are quite willing to allow others to put themselves out on your behalf. Rules and regulations could easily get on your nerves today and it might be all you can manage not to give someone in authority a piece of your mind – this is probably best avoided!

25 SATURDAY
Moon Age Day 8   Moon Sign Sagittarius

am..

pm..

There may be a chance of a profitable development in your life and finances generally look stronger than before, so be open to opportunities. You will need to show a good deal of compromise when dealing with younger family members, some of whom could prove to be in an awkward frame of mind and need careful handling.

26 SUNDAY
Moon Age Day 9   Moon Sign Sagittarius

am..

pm..

It looks as though you need more excitement than your home environment can offer. Although you are a home bird for much of the year, it is around now that you feel a definite desire to get out into the country or, even more beneficially, to the coast. All you have to do is to persuade someone to go with you.

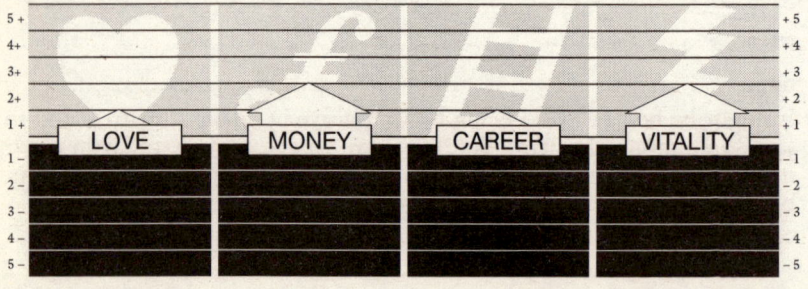

27 MONDAY   *Moon Age Day 10   Moon Sign Capricorn*

am ....

pm..

It could easily feel as if others are getting ahead a good deal faster than you are, and this is actually the case, but only for the moment. Look ahead, plan, and make the most of social prospects, which remain good. By later in the day you should be feeling more like your old self and ready to seek out company.

28 TUESDAY   *Moon Age Day 11   Moon Sign Capricorn*

am ....

pm..

This is a day when you will notice certain limitations, especially within relationships. As always, you are inclined to look at things less sensibly during the period of the lunar low, so the most sensible advice is to take what comes and to avoid reacting as if things are never going to work out well for you again.

29 WEDNESDAY   *Moon Age Day 12   Moon Sign Aquarius*

am ....

pm..

At this time, personal ambitions need to be carefully focussed, though with the lunar low only just disappearing, the chance of actually getting much done in a concrete sense is lessened. Don't allow yourself to become involved in conflicts that had nothing to do with you in the first place. Try to remain optimistic.

30 THURSDAY   *Moon Age Day 13   Moon Sign Aquarius*

am ....

pm..

Things improve and although you are making great strides at work, it has to be through friendship that you show the most positive qualities of nature. People are fond of you – that's plain for even you to see. There is nothing wrong with making use of the fact, if only because you make those around you happy as you progress.

31 FRIDAY
Moon Age Day 14   Moon Sign Pisces

am ....

pm...

With Mars in its present position, don't take hasty actions based on emotional conclusions. If at all possible, you need to detach yourself from specific situations and look at them from a distance. To take such action might appear awkward or counterproductive but this isn't the case. You could be in a very poetic frame of mind.

1 SATURDAY
Moon Age Day 15   Moon Sign Pisces

am ....

pm...

The weekend may bring a change of pace. It introduces less action and a desire to simply sit in a chair and sip on something delicious. The luxury-loving side of the Crab is now on display and it would be hard to deny it any part in your weekend. Think carefully about new ventures before you embark on them.

2 SUNDAY
Moon Age Day 16   Moon Sign Pisces

am ....

pm...

Beware of unnecessary distractions at the beginning of the month and do your best to concentrate on the job you are doing. It is far too easy at the moment to find your mind wandering. This trend will be with you, in one way or another, for a while, though today is the time it displays itself most noticeably.

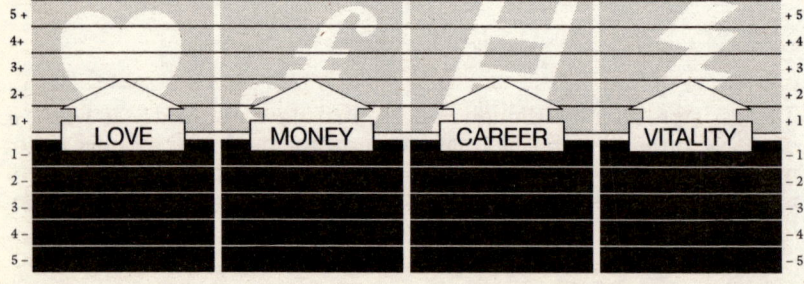

September 2012

YOUR MONTH AT A GLANCE

⊕ = Opportunities are around   ⊖ = Be on the defensive   ⬤ = Life is pretty ordinary

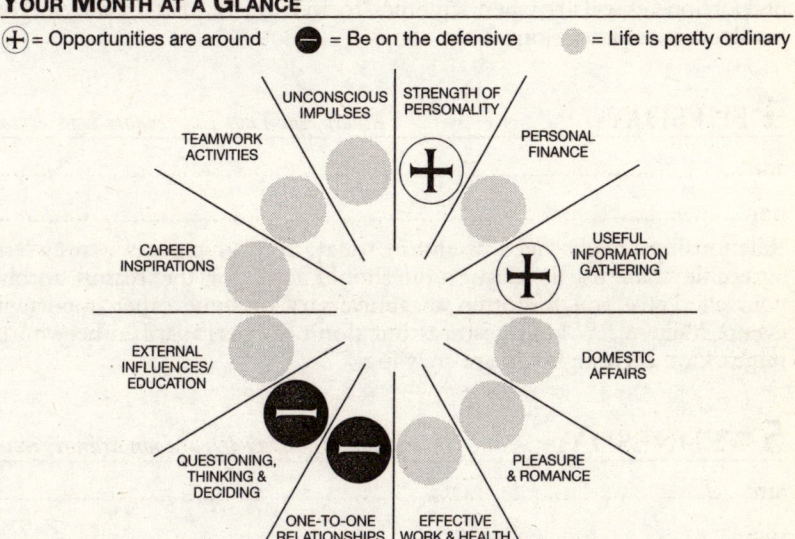

UNCONSCIOUS IMPULSES

STRENGTH OF PERSONALITY ⊕

PERSONAL FINANCE

TEAMWORK ACTIVITIES

CAREER INSPIRATIONS

USEFUL INFORMATION GATHERING ⊕

EXTERNAL INFLUENCES/ EDUCATION

DOMESTIC AFFAIRS

QUESTIONING, THINKING & DECIDING ⊖

ONE-TO-ONE RELATIONSHIPS ⊖

PLEASURE & ROMANCE

EFFECTIVE WORK & HEALTH

SEPTEMBER HIGHS AND LOWS

Here I show you how the rhythms of the Moon will affect you this month. Like the tide, your energies and abilities will rise and fall with its pattern. When it is above the centre line, go for it, when it is below, you should be resting.

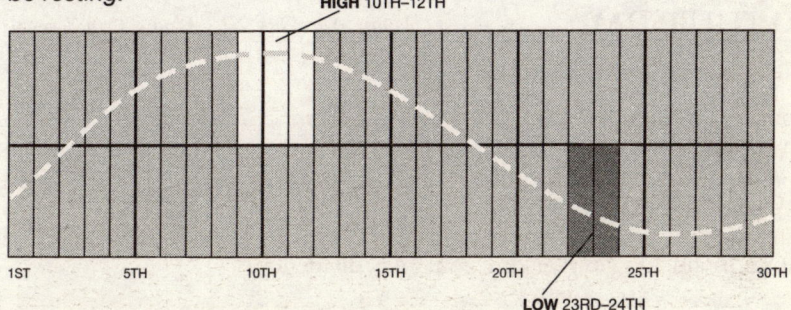

HIGH 10TH–12TH

LOW 23RD–24TH

1ST   5TH   10TH   15TH   20TH   25TH   30TH

3 MONDAY
Moon Age Day 17   Moon Sign Aries

am ....

pm ....

In practical matters, there is plenty to keep you busy and you can expect a fairly good sort of day, even if you may be surprised that not everyone is behaving in quite the way you might have expected. Keep a sense of proportion, especially when it comes to looking at matters that might involve financial decisions.

4 TUESDAY
Moon Age Day 18   Moon Sign Aries

am ....

pm ....

Relationships might need attention today. If your partner proves less agreeable than usual, maybe you should look for the reason within yourself. Have you forgotten an anniversary or some other important event? Make a few kind gestures but don't go overboard, otherwise it might look as though you are crawling.

5 WEDNESDAY
Moon Age Day 19   Moon Sign Taurus

am ....

pm ....

Keep abreast of what is going on. It is very important to be in the right place at the right time today, something you should instinctively know how to do. You should be fairly confident and not half as likely to make unforced errors as may have been the case over the last couple of days. Make the most of good financial trends.

6 THURSDAY
Moon Age Day 20   Moon Sign Taurus

am ....

pm ....

A slightly more progressive phase is at hand and you should have plenty of power at your fingertips to use on those occasions you need it the most. When it comes to forward planning, you are second to none. Give way to the ideas of your partner or to someone you count as a really good and loyal friend and your gesture could pay dividends.

7 FRIDAY
Moon Age Day 21   Moon Sign Taurus

am ....

pm ....

Today should prove to be satisfying. There are things happening in a career sense that you will probably enjoy a great deal. Use the extra amount of charm that you have now to get on the right side of your superiors, but remember not to go too far because whatever actions you take have to be both credible and professional.

8 SATURDAY
Moon Age Day 22   Moon Sign Gemini

am ....

pm ....

Something that matters very much to Cancer is present today: a sense of emotional security. All the same you won't get away from the fact that general situations are changing rapidly. Being quite creative at present, you might find that you decide that the time is right for a new look and perhaps for buying some clothes.

9 SUNDAY
Moon Age Day 23   Moon Sign Gemini

am ....

pm ....

Any form of travel suits you fine on this particular day. Maybe you have a family outing planned, although you are just as likely to gain from a journey that is somehow to do with your work. Being kept in one place isn't likely to suit you at all and you will certainly be happiest when on the move. Restlessness has to be dealt with.

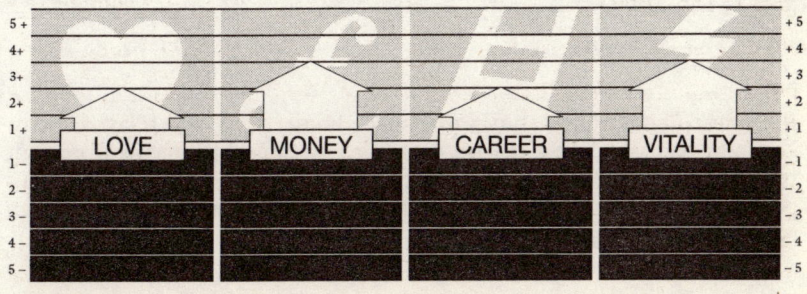

10 MONDAY

Moon Age Day 24   Moon Sign Cancer

am ....

pm ....

The lunar high could easily bring you a day to remember. It seems you can be an expert at just about anything, as you harness your energy and initiative to get jobs done while others stand around and stare. This is a great day to win some Brownie points. Your prestige will be going through the roof all day long.

11 TUESDAY

Moon Age Day 25   Moon Sign Cancer

am ....

pm ....

Things are looking good. Whatever ideas you have had up your sleeve, today is the time to allow them to see the light of day. Ingenious, astute and hardly likely to have the wool pulled over your eyes, you are behaving in a very positive way, whilst at the same time displaying the very best qualities of your zodiac sign.

12 WEDNESDAY

Moon Age Day 26   Moon Sign Cancer

am ....

pm ....

The potential for success remains high while the Moon remains in your Sun sign. Much of the planning that has happened over the last few days can now be acted on. You need to be fairly flexible in terms of the way things get done but, this aside, you are on a definite roll and in a good position to keep things moving.

13 THURSDAY

Moon Age Day 27   Moon Sign Leo

am ....

pm ....

It seems to be the little things that make life feel easy and relaxed today. You may feel a bit like a person crossing a stream but for you at present there are large and closely placed stepping-stones. You should notice this particularly in work situations, probably because your social life is even more instinctive right now.

14 FRIDAY   *Moon Age Day 28   Moon Sign Leo*

am..

pm..

With trends being what they are, it looks as though today continues to be part of a period during which it is not at all difficult to get what you want. At the moment you are silver-tongued and quite able to talk people round with very few problems. Your personality is magnetic and people instinctively want to be on your side.

15 SATURDAY   *Moon Age Day 29   Moon Sign Virgo*

am..

pm..

Life continues to look good and activities are varied. There are plenty of positive highlights around social possibilities, so make sure your diary is full. On the other hand, you may not get on too famously at work; you may possibly be held back by the attitude of others. You can be particularly considerate of people in any form of distress.

16 SUNDAY   *Moon Age Day 0   Moon Sign Virgo*

am..

pm..

It would be good to make sure you are open to new experiences because there are likely to be a number of them turning up around now. Fortunately, you should have plenty of vitality. What really stands out is your ability to communicate with almost anyone. This is not a good day for routine or tedious jobs – leave them for now.

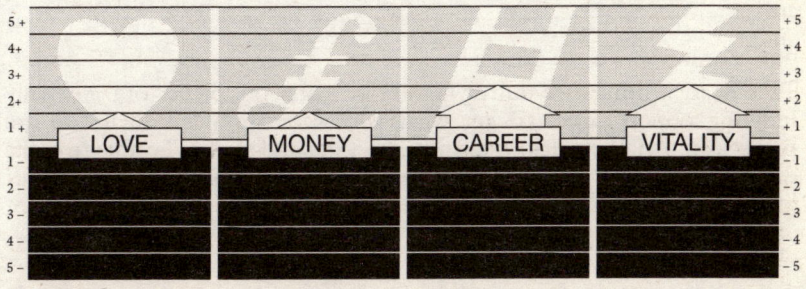

17 MONDAY
Moon Age Day 1   Moon Sign Libra

am ....

pm ....

The position of Venus and Mercury in your chart shows just how much you like to be in the spotlight now, so even if practical matters are on the back burner, make sure social ones predominate. Being noticed positively by people you find attractive is part of the planetary deal now and you should succeed in your mission to turn heads.

18 TUESDAY
Moon Age Day 2   Moon Sign Libra

am ....

pm ....

The Crab thrives on challenges today, especially professional ones. Once you have made up your mind and adopted a specific course of action, make sure no amount of persuasion changes your mind; you'll have the determination to stand firm. Remain flexible on matters where you are less convinced you are right.

19 WEDNESDAY
Moon Age Day 3   Moon Sign Scorpio

am ....

pm ....

As is often the case for you, you will be at your best amongst familiar faces now because it is from these people that most of the positive aspects of life will spring. Although you get on well with strangers as a rule, at present you could find it hard work relating to them and making much headway.

20 THURSDAY
Moon Age Day 4   Moon Sign Scorpio

am ....

pm ....

Take heart if things are dull at first today. Later on, plenty of potentially fulfilling opportunities to get what you want should arise if you are patient. In social settings, you shine like a star and should be able to make quite an impression on people who have some sort of power to make your life easier.

21 FRIDAY
Moon Age Day 5   Moon Sign Sagittarius

am ....

pm ....

Start looking around you because today should prove great for making new contacts. Look out for the possibility of socialising on a bigger scene than might normally be the case and don't turn down any chance to get on your glad rags and have fun. Some interesting news may come along via the telephone or maybe a text message.

22 SATURDAY
Moon Age Day 6   Moon Sign Sagittarius

am ....

pm ....

It is true that there are matters to be faced head on today, some of which you won't really wish to address at all. Being brave and plunging in head first is the best way forward; that way you get things sorted out very early in the day. Later on, you can turn your attention towards having fun, something that definitely does appeal.

23 SUNDAY
Moon Age Day 7   Moon Sign Capricorn

am ....

pm ....

This will not be the most dynamic Sunday you have encountered this year. The lunar low has a part to play in the way you are thinking and acting, and the only way forward is to allow other people to do some of the work, whilst you sit back and watch. This might go against the grain but the rest will do you some good.

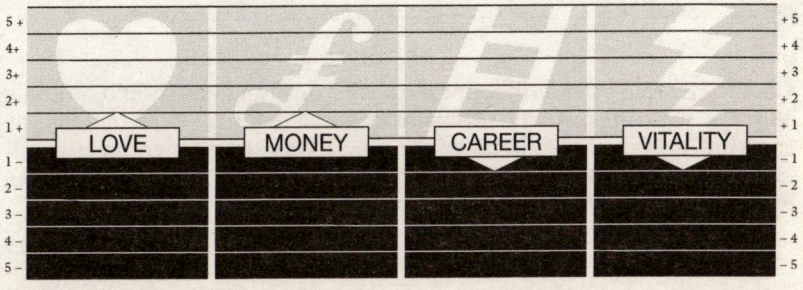

24 MONDAY
Moon Age Day 8   Moon Sign Capricorn

am ....

pm ....

The lunar low is still present and getting plenty of rest would be a good idea today. Let's face it, you have been pushing more than usually hard for a Cancerian recently, so you deserve to sit back and take stock. It won't do you any harm at all and could prove to be a positive move.

25 TUESDAY
Moon Age Day 9   Moon Sign Aquarius

am ....

pm ....

Circumstances in your life are beginning to change and this would be an excellent time to be thinking up new ideas, or even adopting ideas put forward by your friends. On so many occasions, you can help others realise their full potential but right now you have the chance to help yourself at the same time.

26 WEDNESDAY
Moon Age Day 10   Moon Sign Aquarius

am ....

pm ....

Now there is a tendency for you to have to put things right that should already have been done and finished. In some instances, it won't be your fault, but there doesn't appear to be any choice. Even when you know that others have been careless or slipshod, it will be up to you to straighten things out. It isn't fair, but that's life.

27 THURSDAY
Moon Age Day 11   Moon Sign Aquarius

am ....

pm ....

Characteristically, family life appeals to you today and you should be doing all you can to sort out little problems at home that have been building up for a few days. You should make the time to get to know younger family members better, as they mature so quickly. Friends will be welcome, but let them come to you.

28 FRIDAY

Moon Age Day 12   Moon Sign Pisces

am ....

pm..

A long-standing commitment needs urgent attention because it is possible you have put the situation to the back of your mind. You have to be prepared to take chances, especially in monetary situations. At this time, you should not be afraid to take matters into your own hands and be quite positive in the way you speak.

29 SATURDAY

Moon Age Day 13   Moon Sign Pisces

am ....

pm..

Don't be disappointed if some of your plans are waylaid, most likely by circumstances rather than by people. If you suddenly feel you need some excitement in your life, this is the time to go out and look for it. With good creative abilities, you could do much to improve your living surroundings and circumstances now.

30 SUNDAY

Moon Age Day 14   Moon Sign Aries

am ....

pm..

There's no doubt about it: your ability to get other people on your side is strong and you need to make the most of it. Personality issues are to the fore. You might think that you fail to make the sort of impression that really counts, though before today is out you are likely to discover that this isn't the case at all.

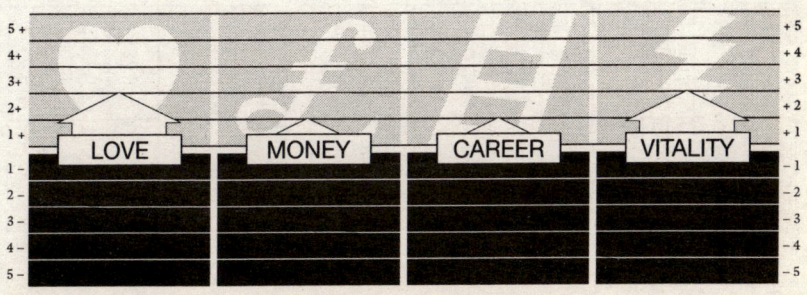

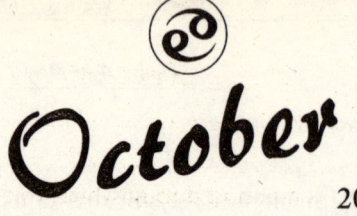

October

2012

YOUR MONTH AT A GLANCE

⊕ = Opportunities are around   ⊖ = Be on the defensive   ⬤ = Life is pretty ordinary

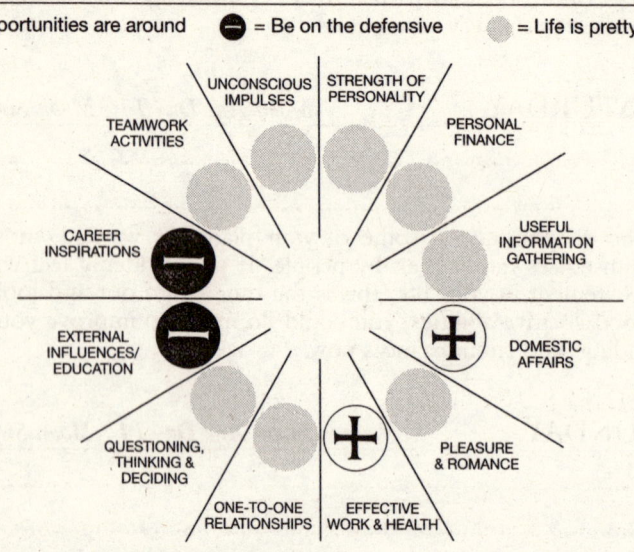

OCTOBER HIGHS AND LOWS

Here I show you how the rhythms of the Moon will affect you this month. Like the tide, your energies and abilities will rise and fall with its pattern. When it is above the centre line, go for it, when it is below, you should be resting.

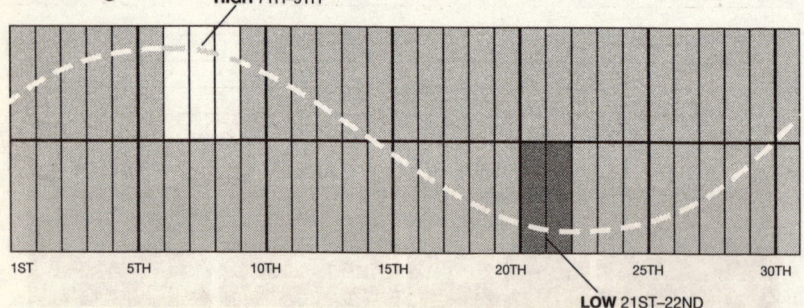

1 MONDAY
Moon Age Day 15   Moon Sign Aries

am ....

pm...

It looks as though this is a period during which you should spend some time thinking about personal matters that need special attention. With a slight pause in the general forward momentum of life and a contemplative mood coming upon you, fairly lengthy periods of concentrated pondering are indicated.

2 TUESDAY
Moon Age Day 16   Moon Sign Taurus

am ....

pm...

You are still fairly pensive and issues from the past are inclined to divert your mind from the jobs at hand. The only reason for this is your present tendency to analyse things too much. Indulge yourself a little early in the day, but break out after lunch.

3 WEDNESDAY
Moon Age Day 17   Moon Sign Taurus

am ....

pm...

It appears that there are few possibilities for having your ego massaged today but you simply have to get on and do things all the same. There could be difficulty in deciding how you want to spend your free time, especially during a period when practically everyone in the family is trying to attract your attention. What do you want to do?

4 THURSDAY
Moon Age Day 18   Moon Sign Taurus

am ....

pm...

Slightly better progress is possible today, and especially so if you are a working Crab. Friends can appear distant, or even awkward, which means you may have to analyse their possible problems. Fortunately, your tolerance level is extremely high and you will benefit from expending the effort to look deep into situations.

5 FRIDAY
Moon Age Day 19 Moon Sign Gemini

am ....

pm ....

As has been the case for a while, emotional issues and the way you view them are inclined to dominate personal relationships whereas you should really be focusing on practical matters. If you can, defuse issues before they take on any real importance and avoid getting involved in discussions you know could be contentious.

6 SATURDAY
Moon Age Day 20 Moon Sign Gemini

am ....

pm ....

Most Crabs would be quite happy to take a break right now. It has been a busy and in some ways demanding week, sometimes without the number of social and personal diversions you need. Some respite comes today and you will certainly want to make the most of all opportunities to find a change of scene as the lunar high beckons.

7 SUNDAY
Moon Age Day 21 Moon Sign Cancer

am ....

pm ....

The lunar high does much to redress a few balances now and finds you more centred in your attitude. Contacts with others are less strained and you show strong diplomatic skills, which you can use to your advantage. When it comes to money, you can afford to chance your arm at the moment and you will also be feeling generous.

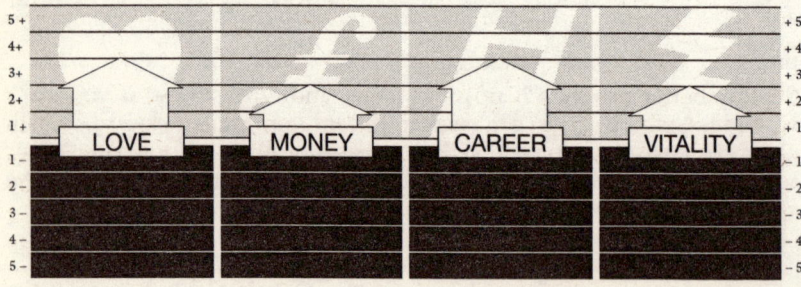

8 MONDAY
Moon Age Day 22   Moon Sign Cancer

am ....

pm...

You should be able to move forward positively now. Without doubt, this is the best time of the month to chance your arm. Although you might be somewhat hesitant with cash, trends are very good right now. The lunar high makes you actively seek out fun, not simply for yourself but on account of anyone who is important to your life.

9 TUESDAY
Moon Age Day 23   Moon Sign Cancer

am ....

pm...

It is often said that knowledge is power. This certainly seems to be the case as far as you are concerned now. You are in the know and you can make it count. The biggest gains are likely to be professional in nature but there are also good romantic trends and these are increased significantly by the lunar high.

10 WEDNESDAY
Moon Age Day 24   Moon Sign Leo

am ....

pm...

It is possible that professional challenges will come along for Crabs who are working hard at the moment. You will be able to make more headway than usual out in the wider world, though you could find stumbling blocks cropping up at home. Respond to the needs of the day as and when they arise because you are very adaptable.

11 THURSDAY
Moon Age Day 25   Moon Sign Leo

am ....

pm...

You are feeling very sociable now and friendship issues are enhanced by prevailing astrological trends, making happiness in association with others much more likely. New encounters will have more to offer you for the next few days and you could find yourself travelling in the company of people you find very entertaining.

12 FRIDAY

Moon Age Day 26   Moon Sign Virgo

am...

pm...

It is possible that in terms of your personal life today, a few of the slight disappointments you could have encountered recently are now being reversed and a much-valued apology is likely to come your way. All the same, everything is not going to be quite what it seems so use a little circumspection.

13 SATURDAY

Moon Age Day 27   Moon Sign Virgo

am...

pm...

It's clear there are gains to be made right now and the material considerations of life must be part of the scenario. The general level of energy you are displaying is only going to rise and that means you should be keeping extremely busy and enjoying a generally favourable time. If you get out and about, the weekend should be fun.

14 SUNDAY

Moon Age Day 28   Moon Sign Libra

am...

pm...

Monetary developments should be an area of growth worth looking at carefully while you have the time. From a social point of view, there are some interesting times to be had, especially if you find a way to mix with some less than likely individuals. What you will yearn for at this time is excitement.

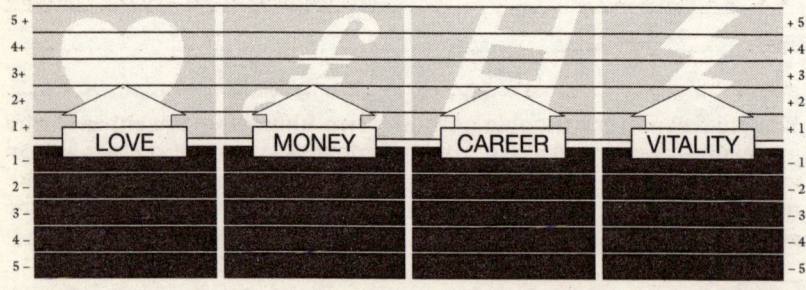

15 MONDAY   *Moon Age Day 0   Moon Sign Libra*

am ....

pm..

It would be good to make sure you are looking and listening at the start of this week because there are situations that could work to your distinct advantage. Routines are easily dealt with, though not necessarily welcome in some instances. If you find you are suffering from a degree of wanderlust, by all means do something about it.

16 TUESDAY   *Moon Age Day 1   Moon Sign Libra*

am ....

pm..

It looks as though you will now decide to get down to the real nitty-gritty of life and you won't have any trouble at all convincing your family and friends that the decisions you make are the best ones in an all-round sense. Love is high on your agenda and you should find exactly the right words to please your partner now.

17 WEDNESDAY   *Moon Age Day 2   Moon Sign Scorpio*

am ....

pm..

Being born under the sign of the Crab you actively like people and enjoy the contact you have with them. This is especially apparent today when you may find that you will do almost anything to be amongst groups and with individuals you find interesting. Avoid being left alone to your own devices.

18 THURSDAY   *Moon Age Day 3   Moon Sign Scorpio*

am ....

pm..

You may have to change your mind about something you thought you understood well but you won't lose credibility as long as you are able to explain yourself. Controversy can dog your footsteps, maybe in terms of your personal life. Real success at this time has a great deal to do with the influence you have over others.

19 FRIDAY
Moon Age Day 4   Moon Sign Sagittarius

am..

pm..

Try to make contact with a variety of different sorts of people as that will make life go with a swing. You cannot afford to hide either your nature or your talents at present. If you are good at something, now is the time to show the fact to the world. Romance could be on the cards for both young and young-at-heart Crabs right now.

20 SATURDAY
Moon Age Day 5   Moon Sign Sagittarius

am..

pm..

As the lunar low approaches, ideas could fail to turn out quite as you had expected and that could mean having to alter your strategy at a moment's notice. This shouldn't present you with too many problems since your mind is working quickly and you don't have too much trouble thinking on your feet under present astrological trends.

21 SUNDAY
Moon Age Day 6   Moon Sign Capricorn

am..

pm..

It looks as though progress might be halted by unexpected setbacks and by pointless worry about situations you cannot alter and might not even wish to if you could. If you find the lunar low is inclined to make you look on the black side of things, give yourself a good talking to – it should be obvious that life is going your way.

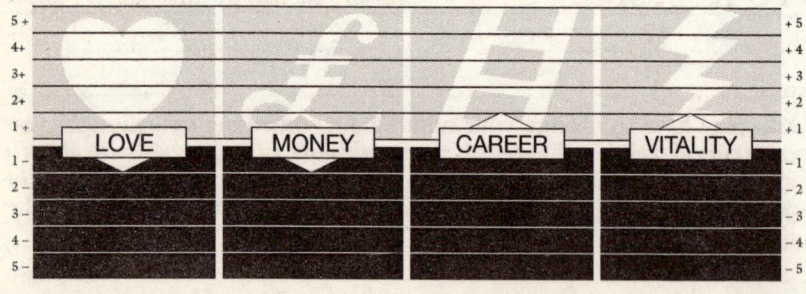

22 MONDAY   *Moon Age Day 7   Moon Sign Capricorn*

am..

pm..

The Moon remains in your opposite zodiac sign and a cautious approach is necessary today, particularly when you are dealing with money. This is not a time to make investments that you know to be risky, nor for putting your name to any document you have not checked very carefully. Friends are helpful but somehow difficult to get at.

23 TUESDAY   *Moon Age Day 8   Moon Sign Aquarius*

am..

pm..

It is possible that finances could be stronger today as you take action to consolidate a position that has been improving for a while. In addition, decisions you took some weeks or months ago are now beginning to pay dividends. Friends could be especially reliant on you at present and you will need to make an effort to find the time for them.

24 WEDNESDAY   *Moon Age Day 9   Moon Sign Aquarius*

am..

pm..

You are in just the right frame of mind to get what you want. You won't achieve this objective by being difficult or pushy. On the contrary, you are sweetness itself and inclined to do as many good favours as there are minutes in every hour. Most Crabs are footloose and fancy-free around this time.

25 THURSDAY   *Moon Age Day 10   Moon Sign Pisces*

am..

pm..

Although it's clear you can gain from the presence of relatives and good friends, associates or colleagues are not quite so fortunate to have around at this time, although you are quite sociable and able to get on well with anyone. Routines can prove extremely tedious, which is why you need to ring the changes when you can.

26 FRIDAY
Moon Age Day 11   Moon Sign Pisces

am ....

pm..

Avoid allowing negative feelings to play an unnecessary role in your life today. Thankfully these won't last long. It is very important not to react too swiftly on instinct for the next day or so but to allow nature to take its course. Long-term plans are sound and should not be ruined by spur-of-the-moment decisions.

27 SATURDAY
Moon Age Day 12   Moon Sign Aries

am ....

pm..

Being born under the sign of Cancer you have a naturally affectionate nature, a fact that could hardly be lost on those you deal with every day. Your warm personality and empathy should be well in evidence today and you can use it to enliven almost anyone you come into contact with. Try to believe strongly in yourself.

28 SUNDAY
Moon Age Day 13   Moon Sign Aries

am ....

pm..

The time has come for you to get new plans off the ground but one or two of them are going to need special help, which you need to somehow source today. A good deal of ingenuity is with you and continues to be your best guide throughout most of today. Look out for romantic overtures coming from someone you least expect.

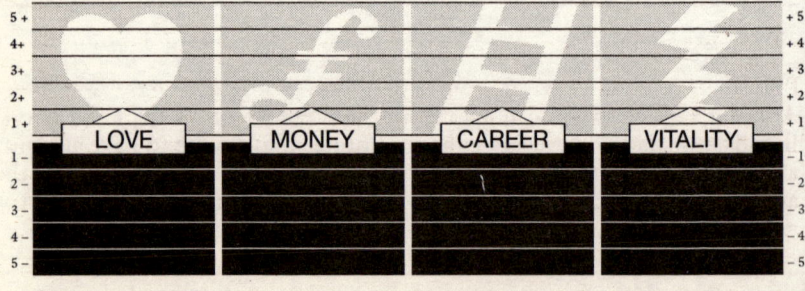

29 MONDAY
Moon Age Day 14   Moon Sign Aries

am ....

pm...

Your self-confidence improves around now and you should commit yourself to what promises to be a wild and wonderful sort of week. Don't be constrained and avoid staying around home all the time. You need fresh air and stimulation, so put yourself where you can enjoy both in the company of influential and interesting people.

30 TUESDAY
Moon Age Day 15   Moon Sign Taurus

am ....

pm...

In both a physical and a professional sense you are clearly 'getting there'. Business negotiations may go particularly well at the moment and might lead to some new involvements you had not been expecting. Don't be surprised if you are singled out for special treatment by superiors and make the most of the chances this offers.

31 WEDNESDAY
Moon Age Day 16   Moon Sign Taurus

am ....

pm...

Despite the fact that the year is growing older, travel seems to be positively highlighted now and you will be doing all you can to find fresh horizons. Although your imagination might not be working overtime to quite the extent that it has been recently, the more realistic qualities of your nature take over instead.

1 THURSDAY
Moon Age Day 17   Moon Sign Gemini

am ....

pm...

There could be a slight sense of urgency about something today, even if you can't quite put your finger on what it might be. In all probability the present astrological trends are making you fidgety, though without any just cause. Try to relax and to enjoy what this rather positive sort of Thursday has to offer.

2 FRIDAY
Moon Age Day 18   Moon Sign Gemini

am ....

pm..

Your warm nature and engaging personality are two of your best assets and rarely more so than now. They can win people round and allow you to take small liberties that might normally be out of the question. Almost everyone loves you at present, a state of affairs that is obvious and which gives you much more confidence.

3 SATURDAY
Moon Age Day 19   Moon Sign Gemini

am ....

pm..

The Moon is now in your solar twelfth house, meaning that your willpower could be slightly diminished. It wouldn't be sensible to expect too much of yourself right now, or to push your luck. Accept and rely on the help and support that other people offer you as most of those around you want to lend a hand.

4 SUNDAY
Moon Age Day 20   Moon Sign Cancer

am ....

pm..

You should be out to maximise your potential good luck today and with almost everything going your way in an astrological sense, this should not be difficult. Acting on impulse is easy, as is adapting your nature to suit that of the people you meet. Now is the time to push for advancement of some sort.

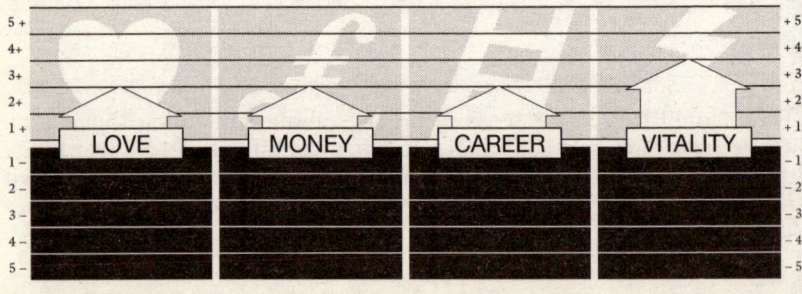

November
2012

YOUR MONTH AT A GLANCE

⊕ = Opportunities are around   ⊖ = Be on the defensive   ◯ = Life is pretty ordinary

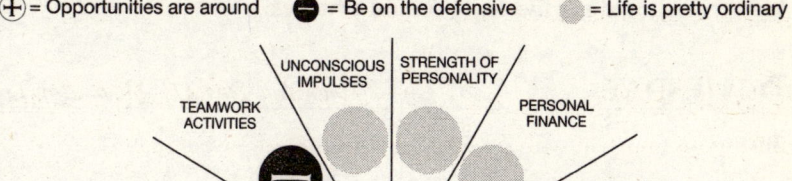

UNCONSCIOUS IMPULSES

STRENGTH OF PERSONALITY

TEAMWORK ACTIVITIES

PERSONAL FINANCE

CAREER INSPIRATIONS

USEFUL INFORMATION GATHERING

EXTERNAL INFLUENCES/ EDUCATION

DOMESTIC AFFAIRS

QUESTIONING, THINKING & DECIDING

PLEASURE & ROMANCE

ONE-TO-ONE RELATIONSHIPS

EFFECTIVE WORK & HEALTH

NOVEMBER HIGHS AND LOWS

Here I show you how the rhythms of the Moon will affect you this month. Like the tide, your energies and abilities will rise and fall with its pattern. When it is above the centre line, go for it, when it is below, you should be resting.

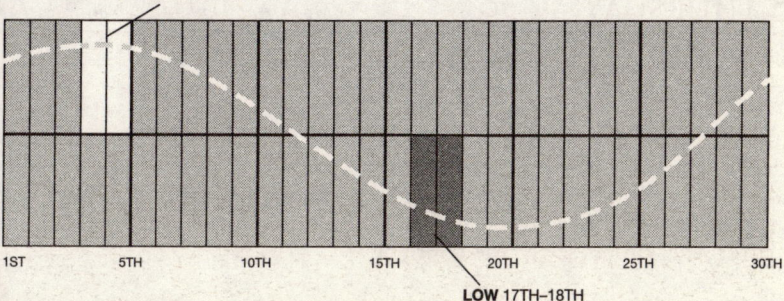

HIGH 4TH–5TH

1ST   5TH   10TH   15TH   20TH   25TH   30TH

LOW 17TH–18TH

141

5 MONDAY

Moon Age Day 21   Moon Sign Cancer

am ....

pm...

It isn't simply a case of your own potential that helps during the lunar high but also the way others can guide you towards significant successes. Don't be afraid to seek out a little help when you need it. Favours are being returned and with your popularity at the moment running so very high, you should get the co-operation you seek.

6 TUESDAY

Moon Age Day 22   Moon Sign Leo

am ....

pm...

Be prepared for money matters to be uppermost in your mind, particularly if you are thinking about a major career change. Keep on the right side of those you know to be in a position of influence and make your talents evident when it matters the most. This might be a day filled with what appears to be a run of significant coincidences.

7 WEDNESDAY ☿

Moon Age Day 23   Moon Sign Leo

am ....

pm...

Such are the influences today that if you need to get a message across to someone you know well, this is the time to go for it. You show tremendous energy and could prove to be quite competitive at this time. Romance could blossom under present trends, especially if you have been looking towards the possibility of a new love.

8 THURSDAY ☿

Moon Age Day 24   Moon Sign Leo

am ....

pm...

It isn't usually like you to be too bossy with friends, especially ones who clearly have your best interests at heart, but there could be a danger of it today. Don't listen too much to gossip because it probably won't get you very far and stick to what you know to be the truth of any situation, no matter what others say to the contrary.

9 FRIDAY ☿ *Moon Age Day 25   Moon Sign Virgo*

am ....

pm...

There are changes to be made in specific areas of your life and now is as good a time as any to put some of them in place. You need to have strong plans laid by the end of the year. Getting what you want from life isn't difficult now if you use a combination of your natural charm and a good deal of confidence.

10 SATURDAY ☿ *Moon Age Day 26   Moon Sign Virgo*

am ....

pm...

Despite the fact that there could be some slight misunderstandings in personal relationships, in a general sense you are getting on well with those around you. Someone might have a very special idea for Christmas that you will be happy to endorse. Confidence continues to grow – make sure you hang on to it.

11 SUNDAY ☿ *Moon Age Day 27   Moon Sign Libra*

am ....

pm...

As is often the case, your present popularity is based at least in part on your sensitivity. You seem to know exactly what makes those around you tick and when to show sympathy. It's true that you are not everyone's cup of tea but that would be virtually impossible. Do give yourself some credit for successes today.

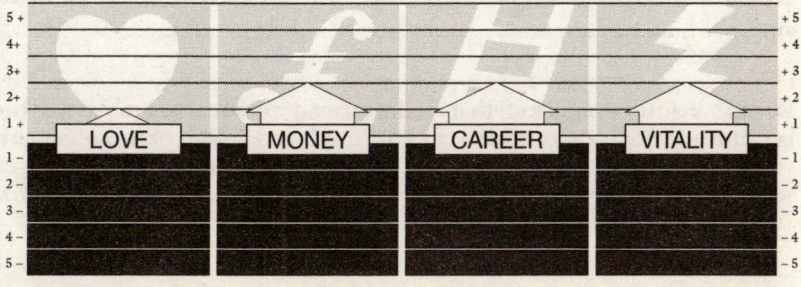

12 MONDAY ☿ *Moon Age Day 28   Moon Sign Libra*

am ....

pm ....

Look out for influences around today that should be much more supportive in a financial sense. Don't be too quick to make judgements about others now and be willing to wait and see in most situations. Someone in the family or your immediate friendship circle could be quite surprising around at this time.

13 TUESDAY ☿ *Moon Age Day 0   Moon Sign Scorpio*

am ....

pm ....

Beware some slight tension that is about now, most noticeably between you and someone with whom you work. Be prepared to show some flexibility. Actually, if you are very careful you can get your own way but without others realising that this is the case. Confidence is present but shows in a low-key way.

14 WEDNESDAY ☿ *Moon Age Day 1   Moon Sign Scorpio*

am ....

pm ....

The generally happy outlook that typifies you brings you popularity today and this should continue for much of the coming week. It should be easy to show just how genuine you are and nobody is likely to doubt your integrity at present. This means that you can put forward your own agenda with a good deal of confidence.

15 THURSDAY ☿ *Moon Age Day 2   Moon Sign Sagittarius*

am ....

pm ....

Beware a little confusion that could attend personal matters, maybe because you don't quite understand the needs and wishes of those around you to the extent you normally would. This all might mean you have to second-guess the way others are likely to behave, which isn't going to be very easy. Start to look at new interests now.

16 FRIDAY ☿ *Moon Age Day 3   Moon Sign Sagittarius*

am ....

pm ....

You don't have to go too far to feel fulfilled at this stage of the week. Although you might have the chance for movement, what matters the most is feeling content with your lot. Some of you will already have your eyes set firmly on Christmas and all that it is going to bring into your life. Forward planning matters to the Crab.

17 SATURDAY ☿ *Moon Age Day 4   Moon Sign Capricorn*

am ....

pm ....

Life could seem rather dull and the amount of progress you are making might be quite limited. In a sense that doesn't matter, because it is how happy you are that counts. The lunar low will bring delays this month and it might take the edge off certain situations but you should remain relaxed so it is unlikely to depress you.

18 SUNDAY ☿ *Moon Age Day 5   Moon Sign Capricorn*

am ....

pm ....

Suspend major decision-making for the moment and be willing to simply go with the flow for a couple of days. That doesn't mean you are giving up on anything – just having a short break. Family members should be good to be around right now and you should take the opportunity to talk through an issue that has troubled you of late.

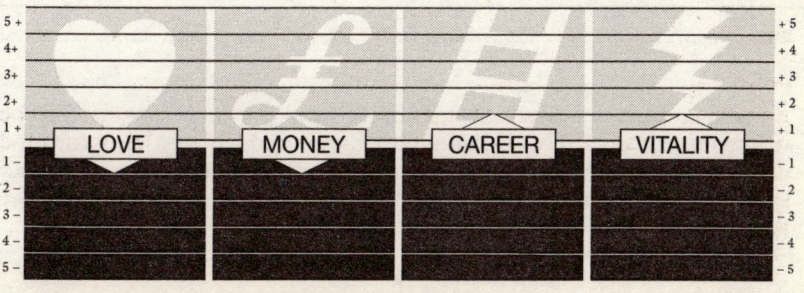

19 MONDAY ☿ *Moon Age Day 6 Moon Sign Aquarius*

am ....

pm ....

You have some very specific talents and it appears that they are really showing over the next few days. Charm is definitely top of the list and if there is anything you have been wanting of late, now is the time to go out and ask for it. No reasonable request is likely to be denied you at the moment. The lunar low is now well out of the way.

20 TUESDAY ☿ *Moon Age Day 7 Moon Sign Aquarius*

am ....

pm ....

In terms of your social life, this should be a very beneficial period. Present influences can bring you into contact with people from many different walks of life. Your horizons will be broadened immensely and it looks as though you have extra energy when you need it the most. Best of all today – romance shines brightly in your life.

21 WEDNESDAY ☿ *Moon Age Day 8 Moon Sign Pisces*

am ....

pm ....

Don't worry yourself over an issue that you cannot alter and go with the flow when there's nothing else to be done. There are individuals around now who genuinely want to help you if you will allow it. Getting to know new people might seem particularly interesting, and this could turn out to be very useful in the longer-term.

22 THURSDAY ☿ *Moon Age Day 9 Moon Sign Pisces*

am ....

pm ....

A personal plan or a specific intention on your part may now have to be scrapped, probably through no fault of your own. If this leads to some disappointment, the best way forward is to forget about a situation that is in the past and to pull even harder for the winning post in other ways. People make a fuss of you later today.

23 FRIDAY ☿ *Moon Age Day 10   Moon Sign Pisces*

am ....

pm...

If you are feeling restless, you might decide that the time is right to take a holiday. You can get a great deal out of journeys of any sort and although the summer is now well over, travel that is organised at very short notice could be the most enjoyable of all. You may also gain from mixing with people who come from far away.

24 SATURDAY ☿ *Moon Age Day 11   Moon Sign Aries*

am ....

pm...

This weekend could be inspiring. Making any sort of important change is likely to be quite easy today, though you may have to deal with the slightly odd behaviour of a few of the people you are having to rely on at this time. Controversy is possible at some stage during the day, even if you are not the one who is inspiring it.

25 SUNDAY ☿ *Moon Age Day 12   Moon Sign Aries*

am ....

pm...

Even casual things you hear from others could be quite enlightening at this time and so it would be sensible to keep your ears open. Gossip is worth listening to and you will also be doing your fair share of the talking. However, when someone has asked you to keep your counsel, wild horses would not make you speak out.

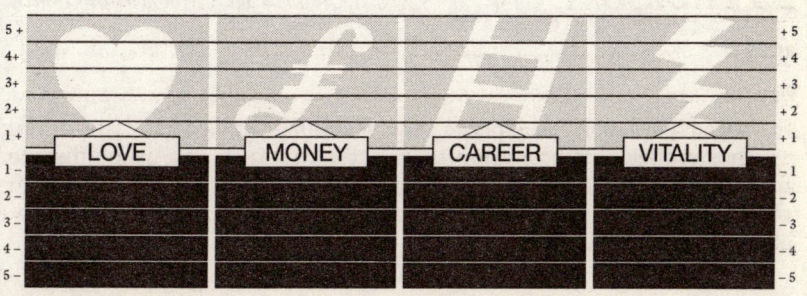

26 MONDAY ☿ *Moon Age Day 13 Moon Sign Taurus*

am ....

pm..

You may be slightly prepossessed today. An issue from the past seems to have a greater bearing on your life than you might have expected. Think things through carefully but don't dwell on them. This is not a good time to get to grips with an important financial issue if you can possibly leave it for a week.

27 TUESDAY ☿ *Moon Age Day 14 Moon Sign Taurus*

am ....

pm..

It would be worth following your intuition wherever it takes you, which could be quite a long way. Despite the fact that the best of the weather is gone for this year, you will be quite anxious to get out of the house and to move around freely. The Crab is particularly inclined towards sports of almost any kind around this time.

28 WEDNESDAY *Moon Age Day 15 Moon Sign Taurus*

am ....

pm..

Any sort of business connection is especially well starred, which would be good for Cancerians who are self-employed. Money could be coming your way from a fairly unexpected direction. Partnerships and the way you relate to others generally are both interesting and important today, so keep your eyes wide open.

29 THURSDAY *Moon Age Day 16 Moon Sign Gemini*

am ....

pm..

In a social sense, you can expect a generally fulfilling period and one during which there are plenty of opportunities for you to shine. Although there are things to be done that don't appear to be satisfying or interesting, you can mix them in with more exciting aspects of life to give yourself an interesting day.

30 FRIDAY

Moon Age Day 17   Moon Sign Gemini

am ....

pm..

This is a time to be acting on the new opportunities that are coming your way. There are trends about that also make it more difficult to concentrate, so deliberately keeping your wits about you is very important. What you won't have any trouble with is finding something to do today.

1 SATURDAY

Moon Age Day 18   Moon Sign Cancer

am ....

pm..

Personal relationships should prove to be quite warm this weekend and might mark the main focus as far as you are concerned. The Crab is feeling quite romantic at present and you should not be slow when it comes to demonstrating the fact. Stay away from the negative influences of friends who are feeling pessimistic.

2 SUNDAY

Moon Age Day 19   Moon Sign Cancer

am ....

pm..

You may find that you can quite easily talk anyone into anything right now so focus on the things closest to your heart and make them happen. When you are at your most communicative, you can overcome all obstacles. Much of the assistance you have been looking for comes your way, particularly at work, and luck is on your side.

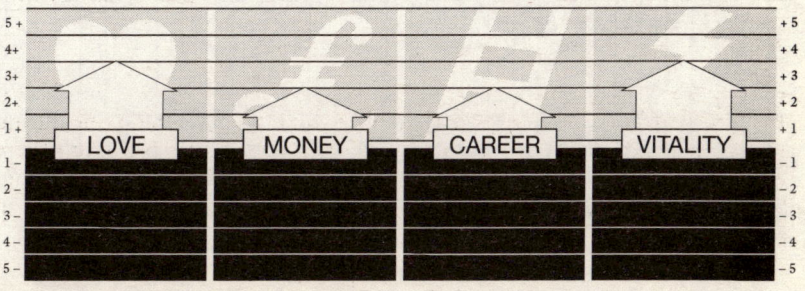

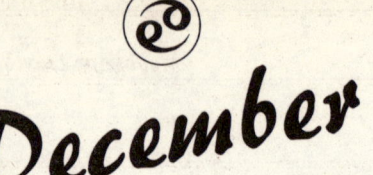

December 2012

YOUR MONTH AT A GLANCE

⊕ = Opportunities are around ⊖ = Be on the defensive ⬤ = Life is pretty ordinary

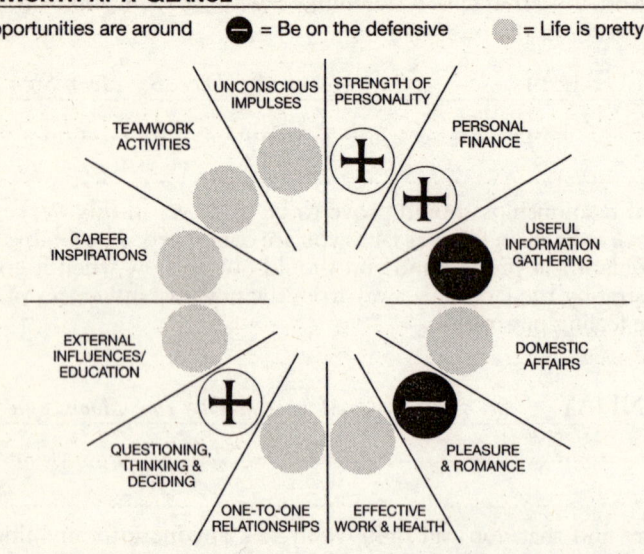

DECEMBER HIGHS AND LOWS

Here I show you how the rhythms of the Moon will affect you this month. Like the tide, your energies and abilities will rise and fall with its pattern. When it is above the centre line, go for it, when it is below, you should be resting.

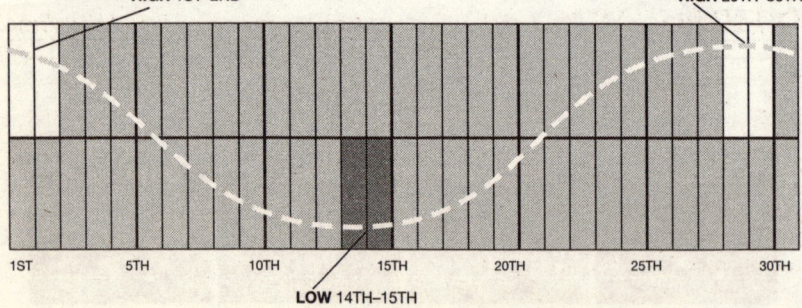

3 MONDAY
Moon Age Day 20 Moon Sign Leo

am ....

pm...

Your luck is in and you should be aiming to exploit it to the full under these trends. People are looking at you in a very positive way and putting a level of trust in you that they may have previously avoided. Christmas celebrations could be starting early for the Crab, or maybe you are just deciding to burn the midnight oil.

4 TUESDAY
Moon Age Day 21 Moon Sign Leo

am ....

pm...

Things are definitely on the move. A hectic pace is probably not only inevitable but necessary today. What matters most is communication. You can talk the hind leg off a donkey, but if you can't find one of those, almost anyone will do! Even people you barely pass the time of day with as a rule are now targets for your tongue.

5 WEDNESDAY
Moon Age Day 22 Moon Sign Leo

am ....

pm...

For many Crabs, this is a day for getting down to brass tacks. Christmas lies just around the corner and bearing in mind the pace of the last few weeks, you may not be properly prepared. Avoid worrying because that won't help at all. Neither will rushing around too much. Be organised and focused.

6 THURSDAY
Moon Age Day 23 Moon Sign Virgo

am ....

pm...

It should be obvious to everyone that your fun-loving side is on display. This is an excellent day for personal relationships and for getting what you want in a material sense. Shopping sprees would be fun and you won't worry too much about leaving a few jobs on the backburner in the meantime. Simply enjoy yourself.

7 FRIDAY
Moon Age Day 24 Moon Sign Virgo

am ....

pm...

Nostalgia reigns today and some preoccupation with past matters is likely. That's fine, just as long as you don't allow events from a previous period to colour your actions now. Experience can be a fine teacher but all too often looking back makes you nervous because you dwell on things that went wrong and not right.

8 SATURDAY
Moon Age Day 25 Moon Sign Libra

am ....

pm...

December is moving fast and this is a time for staying on the move, something you will certainly enjoy now. Don't allow yourself to be held back, especially at those times when you have made up your mind to a particular course of action. Messy jobs, or those that you simply don't fancy, are best delegated today.

9 SUNDAY
Moon Age Day 26 Moon Sign Libra

am ....

pm...

There are still likely to be plenty of comings and goings today, so many in fact that it could be hard to keep touch with everything. It might be sensible to do one job at a time or some confusion could be the result. Your popularity gets higher all the time and you find that a few special people definitely reveal their liking for you.

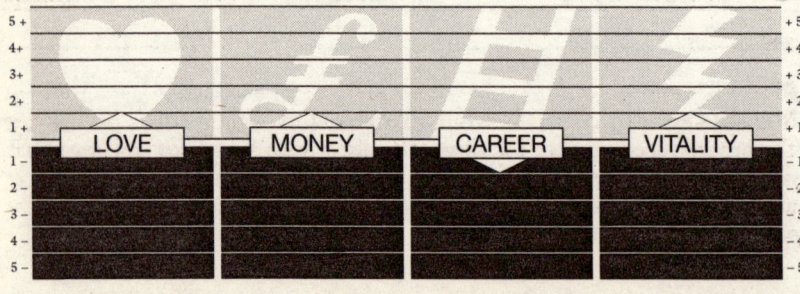

10 MONDAY   *Moon Age Day 27 Moon Sign Scorpio*

am ....

pm..

Professional matters can be a real labour of love today, which is just as well because they are not offering too much in the way of financial remuneration. Be patient, better monetary times are at hand but they are not here quite yet. All the same, some more general good luck could so easily be coming your way around now.

11 TUESDAY   *Moon Age Day 28 Moon Sign Scorpio*

am ....

pm..

In terms of your nature, you are charming and well co-ordinated at the moment – with just the right attitude necessary to get on well in life. You also exude a wisdom that others will recognise so apply it to your advantage. As far as personal and emotional security are concerned, you should find yourself well looked after today.

12 WEDNESDAY   *Moon Age Day 0 Moon Sign Sagittarius*

am ....

pm..

Things should go generally well because in practical matters you tend to keep your eye on the ball. This is not a time to diversify too much and concentration is all-important. If you feel that family members are not taking their own responsibilities quite as seriously as they should, this might be the right time to gently let them know.

13 THURSDAY   *Moon Age Day 1 Moon Sign Sagittarius*

am ....

pm..

You should be on a brief winning streak at work; brief because tomorrow the lunar low could take the shine off things somewhat. For the moment, concentrate on the job at hand and make certain everyone knows you are around. When you score a success, it does no harm to crow about the fact, at least for a short while.

14 FRIDAY
Moon Age Day 2 Moon Sign Capricorn

am...

pm...

With the lunar low present, today is a time for thinking about recent proposals and for following them to their logical conclusion. If you have recently embarked on something that could only really be called a labour of love, you may be about to discover that it can also be profitable. Spend some time with family members.

15 SATURDAY
Moon Age Day 3 Moon Sign Capricorn

am...

pm...

The Moon is still in Capricorn and if there is a problem around today, it could well be your over-emotional tendencies. You would be well advised to use your practical common sense rather than allowing your naturally kind ways to influence your judgement. Someone could be out to take you for a ride, but not if you pay attention.

16 SUNDAY
Moon Age Day 4 Moon Sign Aquarius

am...

pm...

It is likely that this part of December will mark a good time for some sort of professional accomplishment. You could be about to bring a project to fruition now that has been on hold for a while and the chance of making money is quite good. Friends may have special need of your support around this time.

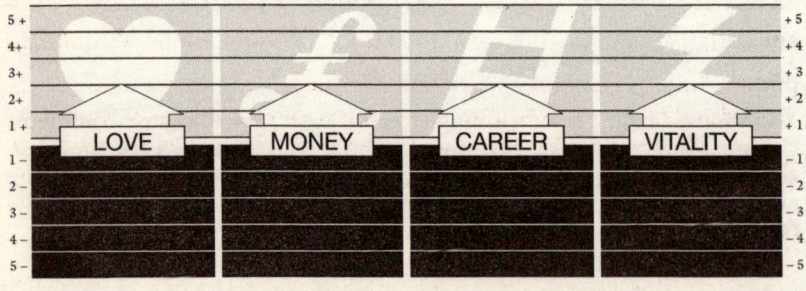

17 MONDAY

Moon Age Day 5 Moon Sign Aquarius

am ....

pm..

With Christmas just around the corner, variety is the spice of life, though it has to be said that you are primarily responsible for keeping things on the move at the moment. Be open to an exchange of ideas that could be quite illuminating and could cause you to modify your own thinking regarding a fairly important issue.

18 TUESDAY

Moon Age Day 6 Moon Sign Aquarius

am ....

pm..

Chances are there are some new and interesting people around at the moment. If you haven't already taken this fact into account, maybe you should do so today. Whether you meet these people at work or in your social life, you can get a great deal out of new encounters. These should furnish you with schemes and plans for next year.

19 WEDNESDAY

Moon Age Day 7 Moon Sign Pisces

am ....

pm..

The Crab is clearly out there in the social mainstream today, even if that is not exactly where you planned on being. At every level, work takes something of a back seat in favour of having fun. Relish the feeling of confidence, especially when you are in the company of people who naturally make you feel good.

20 THURSDAY

Moon Age Day 8 Moon Sign Pisces

am ....

pm..

The Crab shows itself as being very creative in terms of ideas around now, a factor that can stand you in good stead both at home and work. Keep abreast of current affairs as you need to broaden your horizons as much as possible and avoid any situations which could lead you to be in any way restricted in your thinking or your actions.

21 FRIDAY
Moon Age Day 9 Moon Sign Aries

am ....

pm ....

Right now, it is the more practical aspects of life that appeal to you the most. In the main, you will want to do your own thing today and won't take kindly to being bossed around by anyone. The end of a particular phase in your life is not too far away and although it will bring the odd sigh of nostalgia, the gains outweigh the losses.

22 SATURDAY
Moon Age Day 10 Moon Sign Aries

am ....

pm ....

The more ambitious you are, the greater the potential for success. Results you have been seeking for some time will be closer than you think so utilise the tremendous potential around for doing just the right thing when it matters most. You might think there is little time for practical matters so close to Christmas but you'd be wrong.

23 SUNDAY
Moon Age Day 11 Moon Sign Taurus

am ....

pm ....

Both new and old faces come along now, immediately ahead of the Christmas period. You might be deliberately taking a trip down memory lane at some stage today because that is what Christmas is all about. With only two days to go, most Crabs should now be pleased with the arrangements they have made.

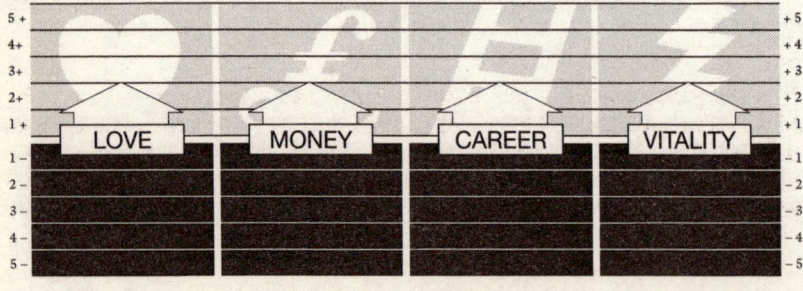

24 MONDAY   *Moon Age Day 12 Moon Sign Taurus*

am ....

pm...

Christmas Eve brings its own form of happiness, probably attached to events from the past. Maybe it's that special decoration that comes out of the box every year that reminds you so much of times gone by? Nostalgia comes as second nature to the Crab and there's no real harm in that, especially at this time of the year.

25 TUESDAY   *Moon Age Day 13 Moon Sign Taurus*

am ....

pm...

It is possible that you may feel a definite need to stay indoors and to soak up the Christmas spirit, but you are still likely to have a particularly good and enjoyable day. Travel is most likely to come later in the holidays. For the moment, you should be feeling warm, secure and surrounded by love.

26 WEDNESDAY   *Moon Age Day 14 Moon Sign Gemini*

am ....

pm...

Boxing Day is likely to be more eventful for most of you and could possibly offer the chance to make a break from Christmas routines and to do something quite out of the ordinary. If such an offer does not materialise, it may be time for you to take control. Stay with people you care about but do new and unusual things.

27 THURSDAY   *Moon Age Day 15 Moon Sign Gemini*

am ....

pm...

It is clear that you are less socially inclined today, probably because the Moon is in your solar twelfth house. This makes you a great deal quieter than of late and more contemplative too. You may have to let close friends or your partner know that you are not sulking about anything and that you are feeling generally fine.

28 FRIDAY
Moon Age Day 16 Moon Sign Gemini

am ....

pm...

Getting into heated debates could be more enjoyable than you might imagine and, with the lunar high now present, you are hardly likely to lose. Back your hunches to the hilt.

29 SATURDAY
Moon Age Day 17 Moon Sign Cancer

am ....

pm...

Get an early start with all important projects and ideas. The more you get done in the morning, the greater the amount of time you will have to please yourself later.

30 SUNDAY
Moon Age Day 18 Moon Sign Cancer

am ....

pm...

When slightly risky situations arise, you can afford to back your intuition, which is extremely strong at the moment. It isn't like the Crab to take great chances, but the ones around at present are calculated.

31 MONDAY
Moon Age Day 19 Moon Sign Leo

am ....

pm...

Do your best to get everyone swinging tonight, no matter what sort of a party you attend. Unless you are feeling off colour it would be best not to ignore the turn of the year and to be with people whose company you enjoy.

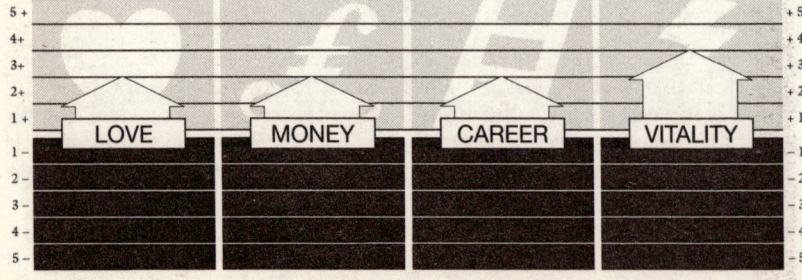

RISING SIGNS FOR CANCER

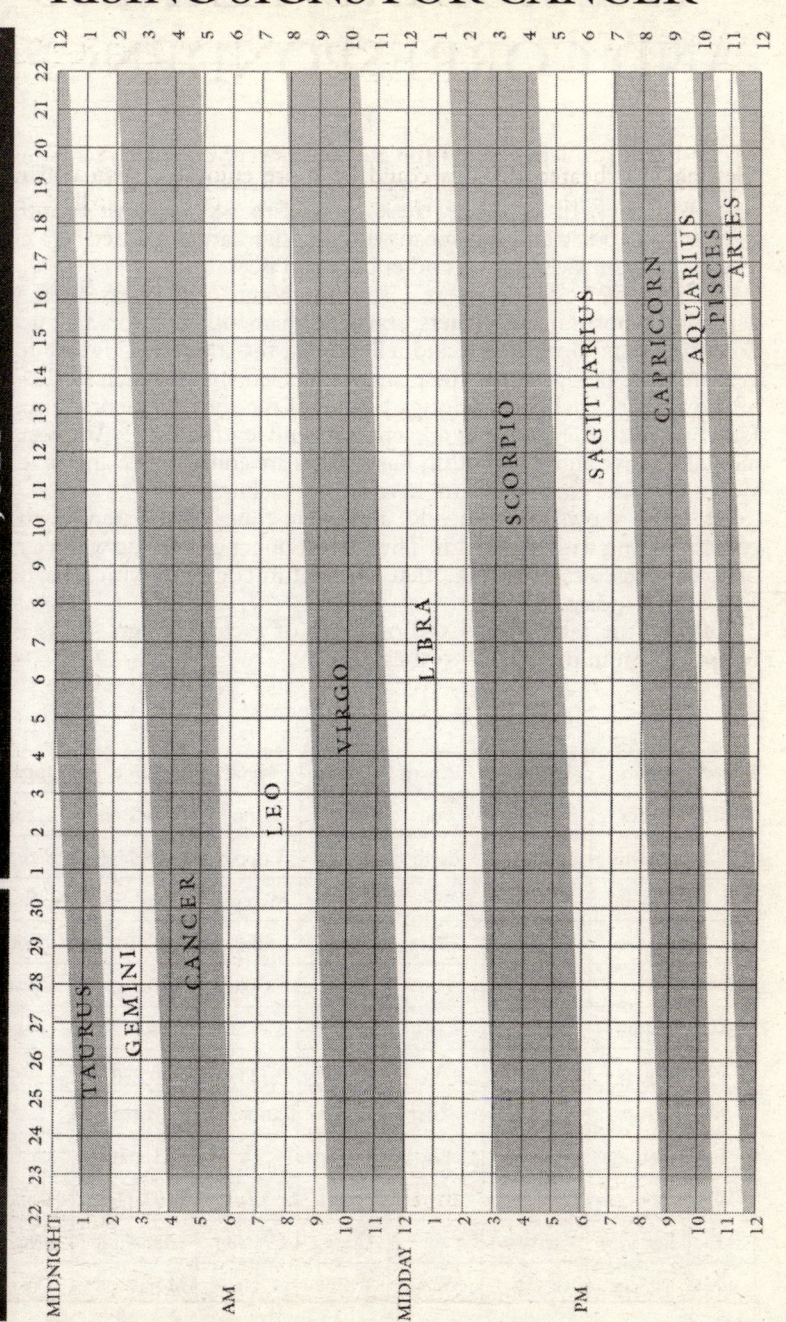

THE ZODIAC, PLANETS AND CORRESPONDENCES

The Earth revolves around the Sun once every calendar year, so when viewed from Earth the Sun appears in a different part of the sky as the year progresses. In astrology, these parts of the sky are divided into the signs of the zodiac and this means that the signs are organised in a circle. The circle begins with Aries and ends with Pisces.

Taking the zodiac sign as a starting point, astrologers then work with all the positions of planets, stars and many other factors to calculate horoscopes and birth charts and tell us what the stars have in store for us.

The table below shows the planets and Elements for each of the signs of the zodiac. Each sign belongs to one of the four Elements: Fire, Air, Earth or Water. Fire signs are creative and enthusiastic; Air signs are mentally active and thoughtful; Earth signs are constructive and practical; Water signs are emotional and have strong feelings.

It also shows the metals and gemstones associated with, or corresponding with, each sign. The correspondence is made when a metal or stone possesses properties that are held in common with a particular sign of the zodiac.

Finally, the table shows the opposite of each star sign – this is the opposite sign in the astrological circle.

Placed	Sign	Symbol	Element	Planet	Metal	Stone	Opposite
1	Aries	Ram	Fire	Mars	Iron	Bloodstone	Libra
2	Taurus	Bull	Earth	Venus	Copper	Sapphire	Scorpio
3	Gemini	Twins	Air	Mercury	Mercury	Tiger's Eye	Sagittarius
4	Cancer	Crab	Water	Moon	Silver	Pearl	Capricorn
5	Leo	Lion	Fire	Sun	Gold	Ruby	Aquarius
6	Virgo	Maiden	Earth	Mercury	Mercury	Sardonyx	Pisces
7	Libra	Scales	Air	Venus	Copper	Sapphire	Aries
8	Scorpio	Scorpion	Water	Pluto	Plutonium	Jasper	Taurus
9	Sagittarius	Archer	Fire	Jupiter	Tin	Topaz	Gemini
10	Capricorn	Goat	Earth	Saturn	Lead	Black Onyx	Cancer
11	Aquarius	Waterbearer	Air	Uranus	Uranium	Amethyst	Leo
12	Pisces	Fishes	Water	Neptune	Tin	Moonstone	Virgo